Large oval basket and melon-shaped basket

C000065280

Instructions on pages 37 (oval) and 73 (melon-shaped)

Fruit basket with braided border and two picnic baskets

Instructions on pages 41 (fruit) and 30 (picnic)

Tray and brown basket

Instructions on pages 54 (basket) and 44 (tray)

Two plant baskets

Instructions on pages 65 (left) and 67 (right)

Flower vase with handles and basket with spiral design

Instructions on pages 59 (right) and 49 (left)

Letter basket and plant hanger

Instructions on pages 71 (left) and 25 (right)

All-purpose basket

Instructions on page 62

Tall round basket and
shallow bowl with handles

Instructions on pages 28 (right) and 21 (left)

Sewing basket with lid

Instructions on page 56

Instructions on page 75

Shallow basket with lace trimmings

Instructions on page 34

Striped basket

Instructions on page 51

Doll-shaped flower vase

Instructions on page 90

Lampshade, donkey and freight train

Instructions on pages 46 (lampshade),79 (donkey) and 83 (freight train)

Small basket with doll-shaped lid and two mirror frames

Instructions on pages 69 (basket) and 87 (mirror frames)

Christmas tree, holly wreath and jingle bells

Instructions on pages 95 (tree),
94 (bells) and 92 (wreath)

PREPARATION FOR WORK

(Actual Size)

Round
rattan

1½ mm
(⅝″)

2 mm
(¾″)

2½ mm
(1″)

3 mm
(1¼″)

3½ mm
(1⅜″)

5 mm
(2″)

8 mm
(3¼″)

10 mm
(4″)

You Min

15 mm
(6″)

Flat
rattan

Center-
scraped
peel

Lunti
peel

About Rattan

Rattan or cane is one of the calamus family which grows wild in Indonesia, the Philippines and other Southeast Asian countries in semi-tropical and tropical areas. Rattan is light in weight, strong and flexible to work with. After being cut and processed where it grows, it is exported to many countries. There are various kinds of rattan used in industry, but the followings are most used in basketry.

Round rattan or center cane, known as reed in U.S.A.
It is cut into various diameters and measured in millimeters; 1, 1¼, 1½, 1¾, 2, 2¼, 2½, 2¾, 3, 3½, 4, 4½, 5, 5½, 6, 7, 8, 9, 10.
1—2 mm are suitable for making small baskets, dolls, animal figures and flowers.
3—5 mm are mostly used for stakes.
5—10 mm are used for frames, handles and furniture.

Rod or Min in Chinese

After the outer bark is removed, rattan or cane is called Min in Chinese. There are four kinds of Min: 30—50 mm are called Tai Tai Min; 20—30 mm, Tai Min; 18—25 mm, Zhong Min and 10—18 mm, You Min. They are bent to shape with hot steam or over a fire. They are used for frames for such furniture as tables, chairs, shelves and screens as well as for magazine racks, umbrella stands and handles of baskets.

Flat rattan

Rattan core or center cane is cut into flat strips. It is used for wrapping and decorative weaves.

Split rattan bark or lapping cane

This is the split inner bark which is left after the outer bark is removed. The width is 2—6 mm. There are two kinds of split rattan bark; one is called Lunti peel and the other center-scraped peel. Both are mostly used for decoration, wrapping the edges of furniture and baskets.

How to choose round rattan

When you buy round rattan at handicaraft stores, be
sure it is flexible, shiny, and round and uniform in size.
If it breaks easily, turns gray, or is fuzzy and not easily
cut into a round shape, then it is not good quality.
These are the grades of round rattan:

Special class . . . . the best quality
First class . . . . high quality and a white color
Second class . . . . not good quality but admired
for its natural color

eached rattan

Half-bleached . . It is soft and used for detailed
weaving.
All-bleached . . . Admired for its whiteness, bleach-
ing spoils the quality of this rattan,
making it weak and fuzzy. It tends
to turn gray and break easily and
is not good quality.

About weaving tools

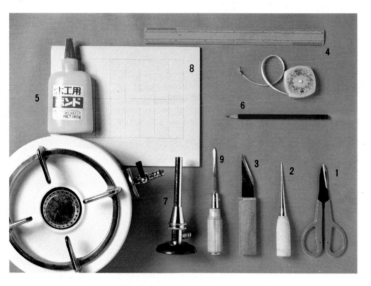

The following tools are used for basketry.
1. Scissors.....Sharp and thin-bladed scissors are used for trimming rattan on
the diagonal.
2. Awl.....It is convenient to use when
inserting additional stakes into the
weave. A sharp awl breaks rattan but
you can use it to make holes in the
plywood.
3. Knife.....To be used for cutting thick
materials.
4. Measuring tape and ruler.
5. Glue.....To be used for securing additional stakes in their places.
6. Pencil.
7. Gas burner.....To be used for singeing
fuzz.
8. Board.....When weaving a rectangular
base, the pattern is drawn and stakes
are fixed on the board.
9. Bradawl.....To be used for opening up
the weave when necessary.

About weaver and stake

The basic technique of weaving baskets is to work weft
or weaver over warp or stake. Choose fairly strong and
thick rattan for stakes and more pliable rattan for
weavers. Hold one end of rattan and bend it with your
finger (as shown in the picture) to check flexibility.

stakes are usually used dry and without soaking in
water. Select them in one of these ways: choose more
rigid rattan for stakes; use stakes that are thicker than
weavers; and use pairs of stakes.

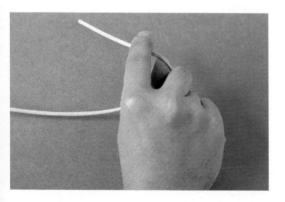

Rattan weavers are generally soaked in water until
pliable enough to use. There is some difference, depending on grade and thickness, but rattan becomes pliable
after soaking about 10—20 minutes in cold water or 5—
10 minutes in warm water. Use the most pliable rattan
for the weaver when starting the round base. It is easy
to weave and the finish will be good.

How to join old and new weavers

When you join a new weaver, lay the old and new pieces on the wrong side. After weaving two or three rounds, trim both ends with scissors as shown in the picture, leaving 1 cm each. Trim ends as short as possible for a smooth surface and a neater finish.

Plain weave with single stakes

join behind the stake

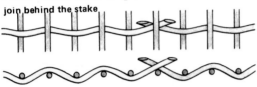

Plain weave with pairs of stakes

join in front of the stakes

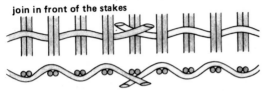

Working suggestions

It is important to keep stakes straight and evenly spaced as you work, for beginners tend to bend stakes to the right. Do not pull the weaver too right, for it causes the article to go out of shape.

Plain weave of under-two-over-two with pairs of stakes

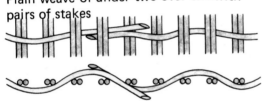

Finishing

When you finish weaving an article and it is still damp, do the final shaping: set corners at right angles, but sure handles are not twisted and that stakes at the edge are fastened well into the border.

Plain weave with flat rattan

overlap

Singeing

If the finished article is fuzzy, singe the fuzz over a gas burner. Hold the article 20 cm away from the burner and keep it moving. After singeing, polish basket with a soft cloth.

Pairing

Three-rod wale

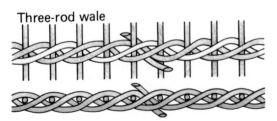

End of weavers after working one round of three-rod wale

Lacquer

Spray clear lacquer over plant baskets and picnic baskets to keep them waterproof.

Care and storage

Baskets in use for a long time may get dusty and need cleaning. Brush them lightly and wash them in soapy water. Dry thoroughly in the open air but not in direct sunlight. Wrap them in paper or a plastic sheet and keep them in a dry and cool place.

Shallow bowl with handles

shown on page 8

This basket is made using basic weaving techniques. It is suitable for beginners to start with. Handles give an interesting look to this otherwise simple basket.

FINISHED SIZE:

15 cm high and 25 cm in diameter across the top

EQUIPMENT AND MATERIALS:

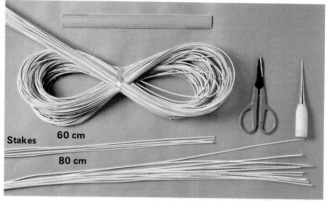

Stakes 60 cm

80 cm

200 g of 2½ mm round rattan, cut into 16 stakes 80 cm long and 4 stakes 60 cm long for handles.

TECHNIQUES: Woven base; Plain weave (Chasing); Three-rod wale and Basic border A.

Woven base

Plain weave over single stakes

(From side)

Basic border A

DIRECTIONS:

1. Base

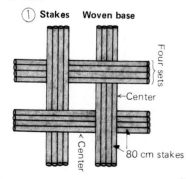

① Stakes   Woven base

Four sets

←Center

← Center

80 cm stakes

oss over four sets of four 80 cm stakes shown, and on the exact center of ch set.

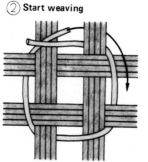

② Start weaving

Choose most pliable rattan for the weaver and work one round over four sets — under-four-over-four. Make sure the stakes are all of equal length, if not, adjust here.

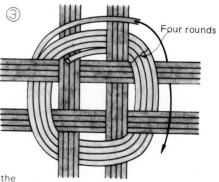

③

Four rounds

Work three more rounds----under-four-over-four. Turn stakes as you weave, so that the weaver is always on your right side.

④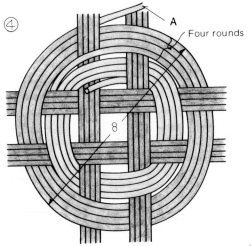

A
Four rounds

8

Work four more rounds, reversing under-and-over of the last round.

⑤ **Chasing**

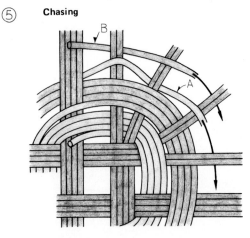

B

A

Separate stakes into pairs. Add new weaver B as shown, then work with two weavers A and B. Take care that pairs of stakes are evenly spaced and laid into a star shape.

⑥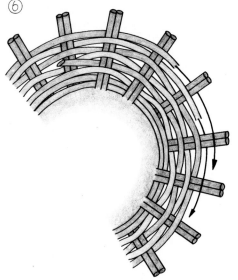

When there is an even number of stakes, two weavers are used in parallel. This is called Chasing.

Separate pairs of stakes into singles at equal intervals.

⑦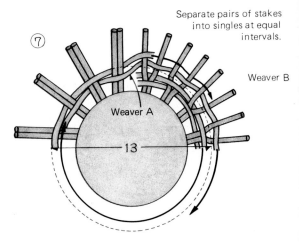

Weaver B

Weaver A

13

Separate pairs of stakes into singles at equal intervals. Continue to weave until the diameter is 15 cm.

2. Side

⑧ Turn over the base.

Bend remaining stakes upward and shape into basket.

⑨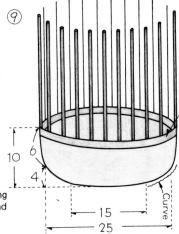

2 rounds of three-rod wale

10
6
4

15
25

Curve

Continue to weave chasing with two weavers, curving 4–5 cm from the base. Continue weaving straight 5 cm more. Work two rounds of three-rod wale and trim ends of weavers.

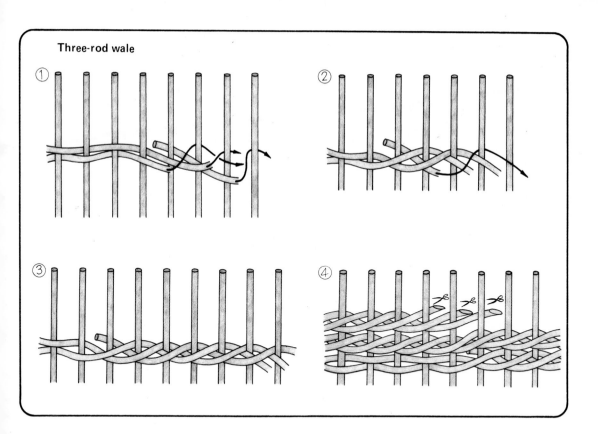

Three-rod wale

① ② ③ ④

3. Border --- Basic border A

Use remaining stakes for border. Soak them in water until pliable. Be careful not to twist stakes when you bend them. This is the basic technique for the border and the one used most since oldest times.

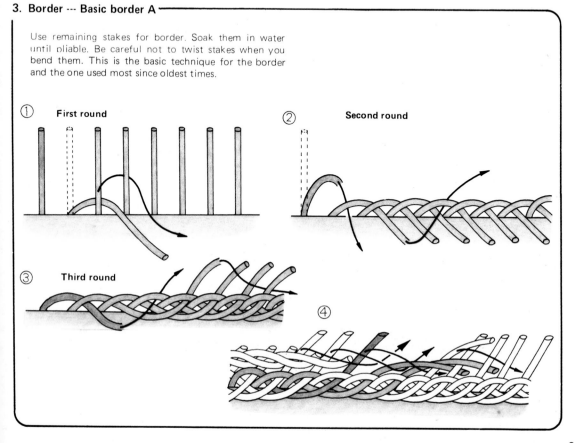

① **First round**

② **Second round**

③ **Third round**

④

4. Handles

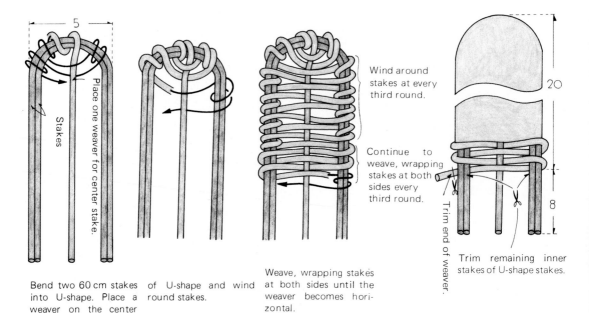

Wind around stakes at every third round.

Continue to weave, wrapping stakes at both sides every third round.

Trim end of weaver.

Trim remaining inner stakes of U-shape stakes.

Bend two 60 cm stakes into U-shape. Place a weaver on the center

of U-shape and wind round stakes.

Weave, wrapping stakes at both sides until the weaver becomes horizontal.

5. Attach handles

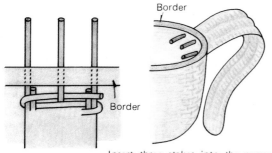

Border

Border

Insert three stakes into the weave just below the border.

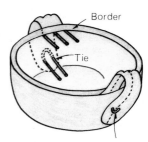

Border

Tie

Bend 20 cm weaver into U-shape and insert it over handle through basket. Tie both ends on the wrong side.
Weave inserted stakes as shown.

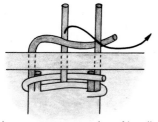

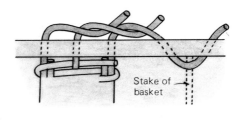

Stake of basket

Insert weaver over stakes of handle through basket.

6. Finishing

While the woven basket is damp (and if it is dry, spray water over it), singe the fuzz, shape and dry thoroughly.

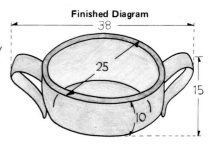

Finished Diagram

Plant hanger

shown on page 6

Hang it anywhere you like. You may also use it as a container for small things. Make hanger with cotton cord in your favorite color.

FINISHED SIZE:

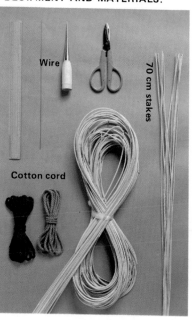

110 cm high including hanger and fringe and 17 cm in diameter across the top.

EQUIPMENT AND MATERIALS.

Wire

70 cm stakes

Cotton cord

150 g of 2½ mm round rattan, cut into 10 stakes 70 cm long
Olive green and brown cotton cord, 7.2 m each.

TECHNIQUES:

Overlaid cross base; Plain weave;
Three-rod wale; Basic border A;
Ring and Turk's head (for ring).

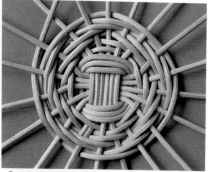

Overlaid cross base.
Pattern of over-two-under-two.

Plain weave

DIRECTIONS:
1. Base

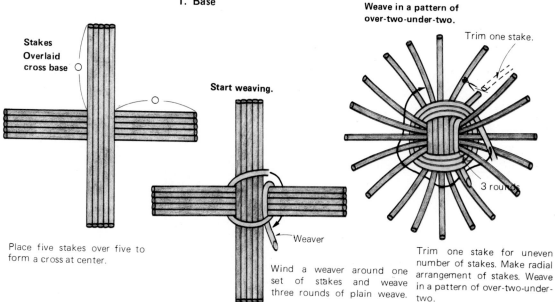

Stakes
Overlaid
cross base

Place five stakes over five to form a cross at center.

Start weaving.

Weaver

Wind a weaver around one set of stakes and weave three rounds of plain weave.

Weave in a pattern of over-two-under-two.

Trim one stake.

3 rounds

Trim one stake for uneven number of stakes. Make radial arrangement of stakes. Weave in a pattern of over-two-under-two.

25

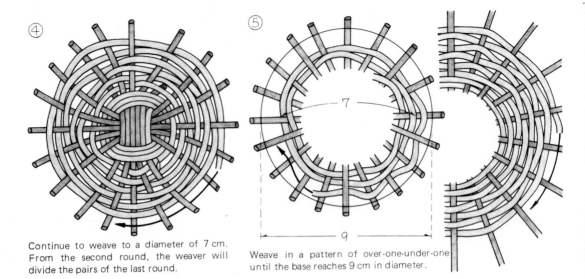

④ Continue to weave to a diameter of 7 cm. From the second round, the weaver will divide the pairs of the last round.

⑤ Weave in a pattern of over-one-under-one until the base reaches 9 cm in diameter.

2. Side

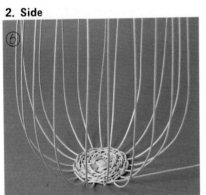

⑥ Bend stakes upward and shape them with your fingers.

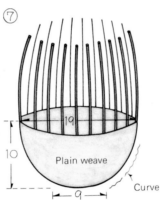

⑦ Continue to weave over-one-under-one, curving as you work.

Plain weave

Curve

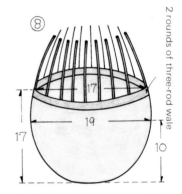

⑧ Continue to weave, bending stakes inward. Work two rounds of three-rod wale (see page 23), adding two more weavers.

2 rounds of three-rod wale

3. Border

Soak remaining stakes in water until pliable and finish the edge with basic border A (see page 23).

4. Ring for hanging

The ring is made by wrapping core with weaver.

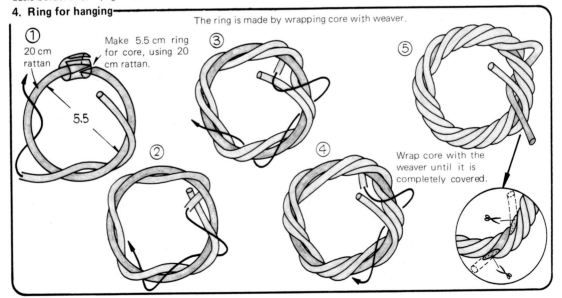

① 20 cm rattan — Make 5.5 cm ring for core, using 20 cm rattan. 5.5

⑤ Wrap core with the weaver until it is completely covered.

5. Turk's head

Make Turk's head for a ring. Make small head, 3.5 cm in diameter (four rounds) and big one, 5 cm in diameter (five rounds) following the 7 stages in the diagram.

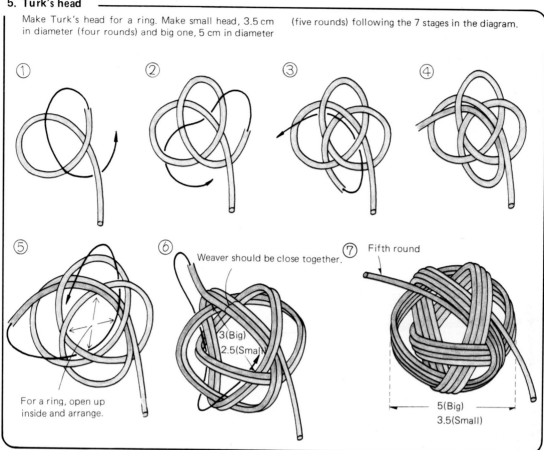

① ② ③ ④

⑤ For a ring, open up inside and arrange.

⑥ Weaver should be close together.
3(Big)
2.5(Small)

⑦ Fifth round
5(Big)
3.5(Small)

6. Hanging rope and finishing

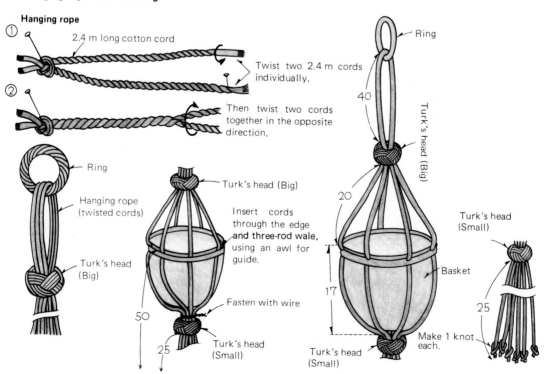

Hanging rope

① 2.4 m long cotton cord
Twist two 2.4 m cords individually.

② Then twist two cords together in the opposite direction.

Ring
Hanging rope (twisted cords)
Turk's head (Big)

Turk's head (Big)
Insert cords through the edge and three-rod wale, using an awl for guide.
Fasten with wire
Turk's head (Small)
50
25

Ring
40
Turk's head (Big)
20
17
Basket
Turk's head (Small)

Turk's head (Small)
25
Make 1 knot each.

Tall round basket

shown on page 8

This article is also made with basic weaving techniques. Practice weaving straight sides, using two weavers over pairs of stakes. Take care not to curve stakes.

FINISHED SIZE:

38 cm high including handle and 24 cm in diameter across the top

EQUIPMENT AND MATERIALS:

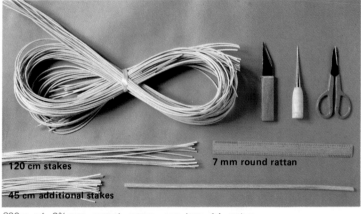

120 cm stakes

45 cm additional stakes

7 mm round rattan

380 g of 2¾ mm round rattan, cut into 14 stakes 120 cm long and 27 additional stakes 45 cm long. One length of 7 mm round rattan, 50 cm long.

TECHNIQUES: Overlaid cross base; Under-two-over-two; Three-rod wale; Plain weave (with two weavers and pairs of stakes) and Basic border A with pairs of stakes.

Overlaid cross base
Under-two-over-two

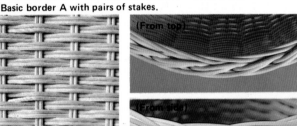

Plain weave with 2 weavers

Basic border with 2 weavers

DIRECTIONS:

1. Base

① Trim one stake.

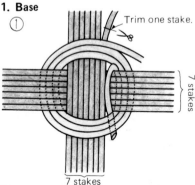

7 stakes

7 stakes

Place seven stakes over seven to form a cross. Weave three rounds and trim one stake.

②

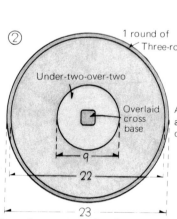

Under-two-over-two

Overlaid cross base

9

22

23

Weave in a pattern of under-two-over-two (see page 25) to a diameter of 9 cm. Weave in a pattern of under-one-over-one to a diameter of 22 cm.

③

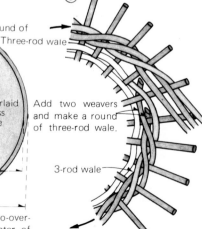

1 round of Three-rod wale

Add two weavers and make a round of three-rod wale.

3-rod wale

5. Finishing
Turk's head (see page 27).

Use the remaining weaver for attaching.

2 rounds of 3-rod wale

Pass the remaining weaver through the back of turk's head.

Center stakes

3.5

Work five rounds.

Four-plait
(Make a button loop with four-plait.)

Center of cover

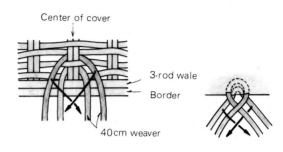

3-rod wale

Border

40cm weaver

Attach the cover
Insert weaver between border & 3-rod wale.

Cover (Inside)

Back (Inside)

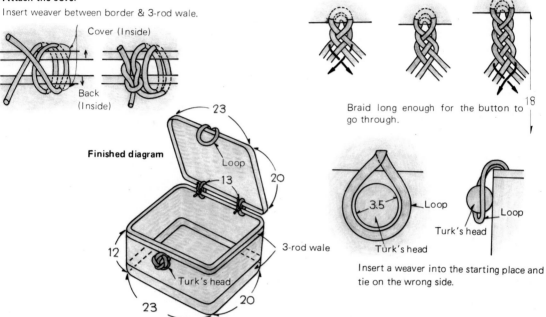

Finished diagram

23

Loop

13

20

12

3-rod wale

23

20

Turk's head

Braid long enough for the button to go through.

18

3.5

Loop

Turk's head

Loop

Turk's head

Loop

Insert a weaver into the starting place and tie on the wrong side.

For the small basket:
Make the small basket in the same manner as the large one, using thinner round rattan.

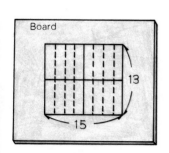

Board

13

15

Stakes

<Basket>

22

57

13

22

<Cover>

14

13

41

14

Finished diagram

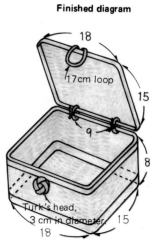

18

17cm loop

15

9

8

Turk's head, 3 cm in diameter

15

18

Shallow basket with lace trimmings

shown on page 11

This is a basic oval basket. It is decorated with lace. Choose the lace in your favorite color.

FINISHED SIZE:

22 cm x 30 cm oval and 21 cm high including handle

EQUIPMENT AND MATERIALS:

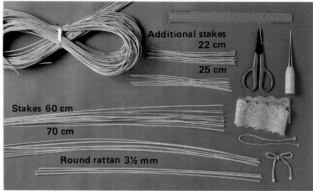

Additional stakes
22 cm
25 cm
Stakes 60 cm
70 cm
Round rattan 3½ mm

170 g of 2½ mm round rattan, cut into 6 stakes 70 cm long, 14 stakes 60 cm long, 8 additional stakes 25 cm long and 16 additional stakes 22 cm long. 3 pieces of 3½ mm round rattan, 55 cm long. Lace, 6 cm wide by 2 m long. 2 cotton cords, 3.5 cm in diameter and 35 cm long, each.

TECHNIQUES:

Oval base A;
Chasing and Rolled border (double border).

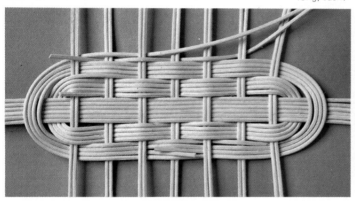

Oval base A

(From top)

(From side)   Rolled border

DIRECTIONS:

1. Base
Oval base A.

Finished diagram

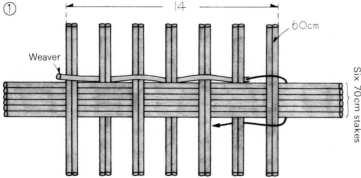

①

14

60cm

Weaver

Six 70cm stakes

Place six 70 cm stakes lengthwise. Place pairs of 60 cm stakes over and under 70 cm stakes at equal intervals. Weave four rounds, pressing the stakes.

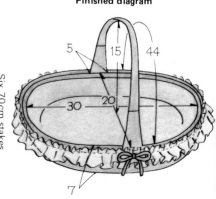

5   15   44

30   20

7

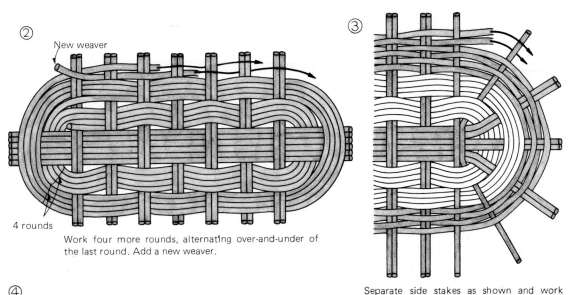

② New weaver

4 rounds

Work four more rounds, alternating over-and-under of the last round. Add a new weaver.

③

Separate side stakes as shown and work 3.5 cm in chasing.

④ 25 cm additional stakes

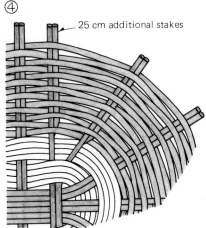

Insert 25 cm additional stakes next to single stakes.

⑤ 1 round of 3-rod wale

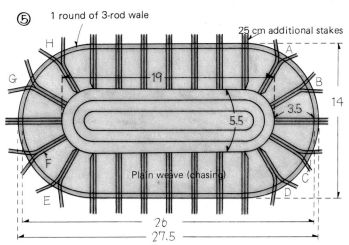

25 cm additional stakes

H

G

19

14

F

5.5

3.5

A

B

C

D

E

Plain weave (chasing)

26
27.5

Separate stakes from A to H into singles.
Add a new weaver and work one round of three-rod wale.

2. Side

Turn over the base.

⑥

20

30

22

Stakes

5

27.5

Bend stakes upward in shape for basket.

⑦

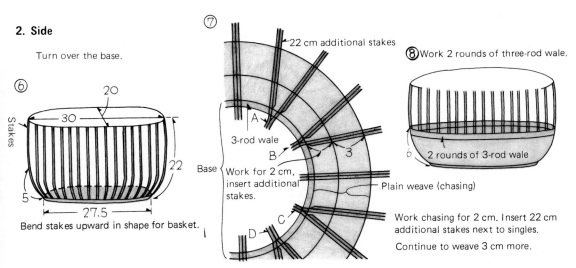

22 cm additional stakes

A

3-rod wale

B

3

Base { Work for 2 cm, insert additional stakes.

C

D

Plain weave (chasing)

⑧ Work 2 rounds of three-rod wale.

2 rounds of 3-rod wale

Work chasing for 2 cm. Insert 22 cm additional stakes next to singles.

Continue to weave 3 cm more.

3. Border ---Rolled border

1st row: Cut 2½ mm round rattan for core to the length of basket circumference plus 5 cm. Place this rattan outside of stakes close to the edge and wind each stake around the core.

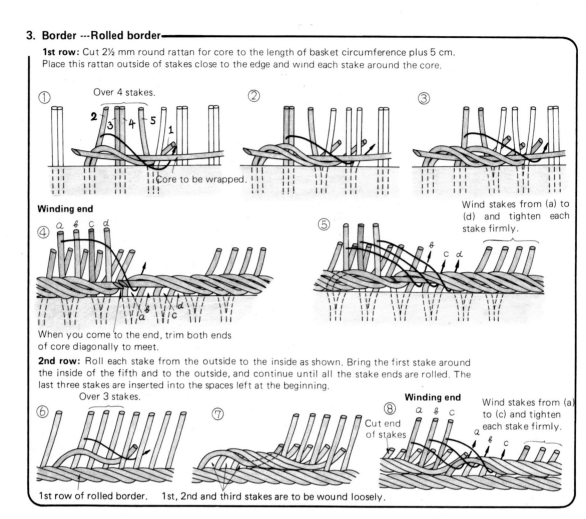

① Over 4 stakes.
2 3 4 5 1
Core to be wrapped.

②

③

Wind stakes from (a) to (d) and tighten each stake firmly.

Winding end

④ a b c d

⑤ b c d

When you come to the end, trim both ends of core diagonally to meet.

2nd row: Roll each stake from the outside to the inside as shown. Bring the first stake around the inside of the fifth and to the outside, and continue until all the stake ends are rolled. The last three stakes are inserted into the spaces left at the beginning.

Over 3 stakes.

⑥

⑦

Cut end of stakes

⑧ **Winding end**
a b c

Wind stakes from (a) to (c) and tighten each stake firmly.

a b c

1st row of rolled border.   1st, 2nd and third stakes are to be wound loosely.

4. Handle

Use three pieces of 3½ mm round rattan for core.

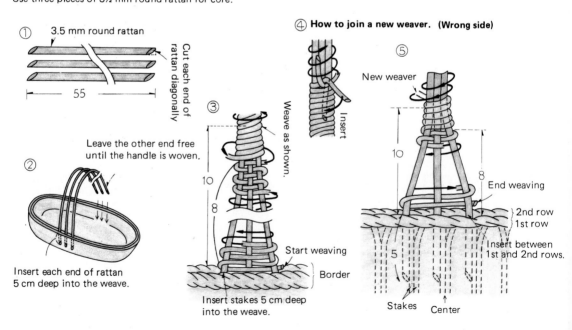

① 3.5 mm round rattan

Cut each end of rattan diagonally

|— 55 —|

Leave the other end free until the handle is woven.

② Insert each end of rattan 5 cm deep into the weave.

③ Weave as shown.

10

8

Start weaving

Insert stakes 5 cm deep into the weave.

Border

④ **How to join a new weaver. (Wrong side)**

Insert

⑤ New weaver

10

8

End weaving

2nd row
1st row

Insert between 1st and 2nd rows.

5

Stakes   Center

5. Lace trimmings

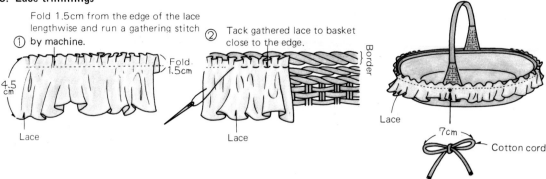

① Fold 1.5cm from the edge of the lace lengthwise and run a gathering stitch by machine.

Fold 1.5cm

Lace

4.5 cm

② Tack gathered lace to basket close to the edge.

Lace

Border

Lace

7cm

Cotton cord

Large oval basket

shown on page 1

This is also a basic oval basket, but you may have a little difficulty weaving with 5 mm-thick rattan. Make this basket after you have practiced basket weaving.

Preparation: Choose 2nd class rattan which is more pliable. Use rigid rattan for stakes. Soak weavers in hot water for more than 30 minutes or until pliable. Trim the ends of stakes on a diagonal and insert into the weave using a bradawl for guide.

EQUIPMENT AND MATERIALS:

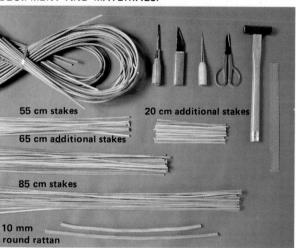

55 cm stakes

65 cm additional stakes

20 cm additional stakes

85 cm stakes

10 mm round rattan

FINISHED SIZE:

44

48 cm long and 60 cm wide oval at the top, and 44 cm high including handle.

1500 g of 5 mm round rattan (2nd class), cut into 10 stakes 55 cm long and 20 additional stakes 20 cm long for base, and 40 stakes 85 cm long and 40 additional stakes 65 cm long for side. One length of 10 mm round rattan for handle, 130 cm long.

TECHNIQUES: Inserted cross base; Oval base B (Packing) **Chasing and Basic border B.**

Cross base

Oval base B

(From top)

(From side)

Basic border B (2 weavers)

1. Base --- Inserted cross base.

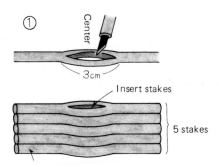

Make 3 cm slits in the middle of 55 cm stakes with knife. Place five stakes lengthwise.

DIRECTIONS:

When you make a large basket like this, trim the remaining stakes after making the base. Then add new stakes for side.

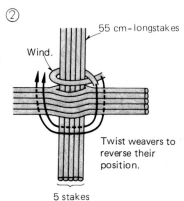

Twist weavers to reverse their position.

Insert five stakes in slits to form a cross. Choose most pliable rattan for a weave and fold in half, wrapping inserted stakes with folded weaver as shown.

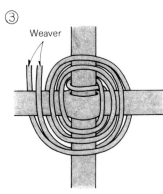

Work two rounds of pairing, pressing stakes tightly.

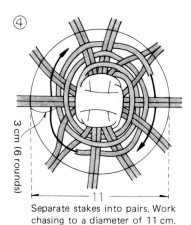

Separate stakes into pairs. Work chasing to a diameter of 11 cm.

Separate pairs of stakes into singles. Continue to weave chasing to a diameter of 25 cm.

⑥ **Oval base B Packing**

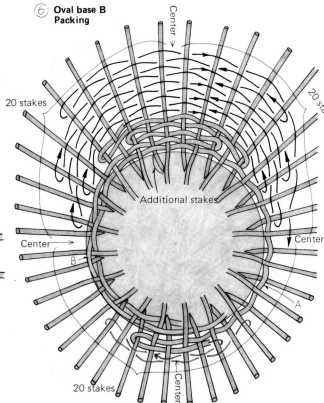

Insert additional stakes at the left of each original stake. Then weave packing as shown, using two weavers of A and B individually.

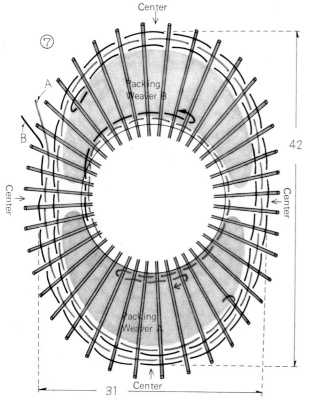

⑦

Center

Packing
Weaver B

A

B

Center

Center

Packing
Weaver A

Center

42

31

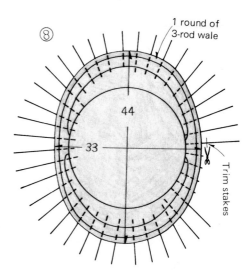

⑧

1 round of
3-rod wale

44

33

Trim stakes

Weave chasing with two weavers of A and B until the base reaches 31 cm x 42 cm oval. Add a new weaver and work one round of three-rod wale. Trim all remaining stakes close to the three-rod wale.

2. Side

Turn over the base.

⑨

Insert side stakes to the left of each base stake into 5 cm deep.
deep.

Base stake

5

⑩

Bend side stakes upward.

⑪

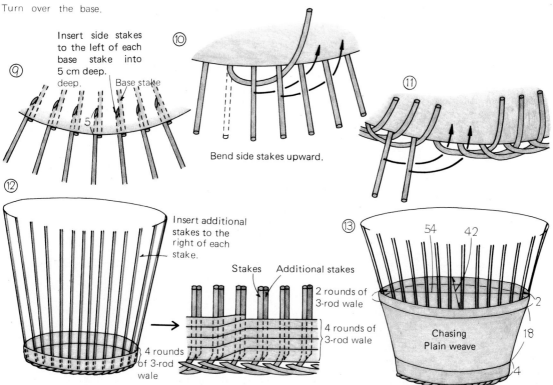

⑫

Insert additional stakes to the right of each stake.

Stakes   Additional stakes

4 rounds of 3-rod wale

2 rounds of 3-rod wale

4 rounds of 3-rod wale

Work four rounds of three-rod wale. Insert additional side stakes next to the right of each stake.

⑬

54   42

2

18

4

Chasing
Plain weave

Work chasing for 18 cm, bending stakes outward. Work two rounds of three-rod wale.

3. Border --- Basic border B

Soak the remaining stakes in hot water for about 30 minutes. Hammer the edge of three-rod wale lightly.
Finish the basket with basic border B as shown.

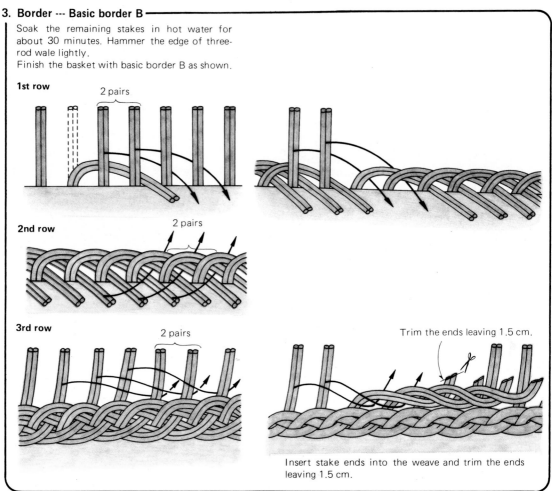

1st row

2 pairs

2nd row

2 pairs

3rd row

2 pairs

Trim the ends leaving 1.5 cm.

Insert stake ends into the weave and trim the ends leaving 1.5 cm.

4. Handle
Cut 10 mm round rattan into 70 cm and 60 cm lengths.

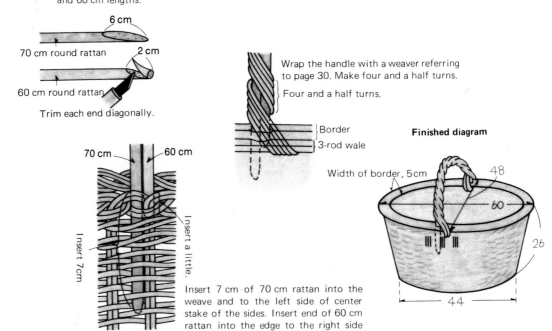

6 cm

70 cm round rattan

2 cm

60 cm round rattan

Trim each end diagonally.

70 cm

60 cm

Insert 7 cm

Insert a little.

Insert 7 cm of 70 cm rattan into the weave and to the left side of center stake of the sides. Insert end of 60 cm rattan into the edge to the right side of 70 cm rattan.

Wrap the handle with a weaver referring to page 30. Make four and a half turns.

Four and a half turns.

Border

3-rod wale

Finished diagram

Width of border, 5 cm

48

60

26

44

Basket with braided border

shown on page 2

This basket is decorated with Tyrolean tape. You may change the width of the open work depending on the width of the tape.

FINISHED SIZE:

30 cm high including handle and 35 cm in diameter across the top.

Three-rod wale; Open work; Pairing and Braided border.

EQUIPMENT AND MATERIALS:

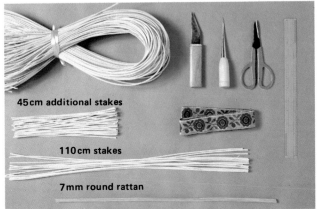

45 cm additional stakes

110 cm stakes

7 mm round rattan

300 g of 3 mm half bleached round rattan, cut into 18 stakes 110 cm long and 36 additional stakes 45 cm long. One length of 7 mm round rattan for handle, 55 cm long. Tyrolean tape, 3.5 cm wide by 100 cm long.

Base   Double cross base

Open work

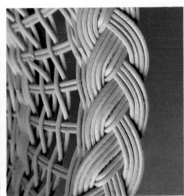

Braided border

DIRECTIONS:

1. Base

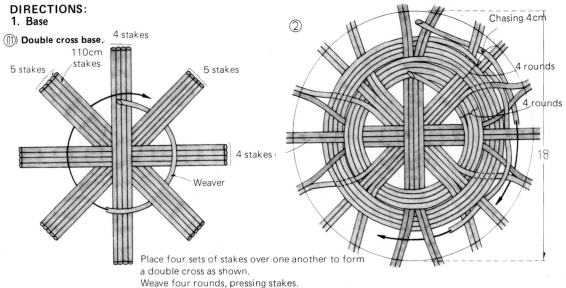

Place four sets of stakes over one another to form a double cross as shown.
Weave four rounds, pressing stakes.

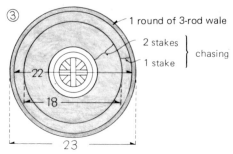

③

1 round of 3-rod wale

2 stakes } chasing
1 stake

22

18

23

Add a new weaver and work chasing, followed by one round of three-rod wale.

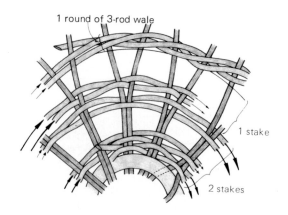

1 round of 3-rod wale

1 stake

2 stakes

2. Side

Turn over the base.

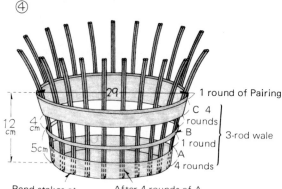

④

29

1 round of Pairing

C 4 rounds
B 1 round   } 3-rod wale
A 4 rounds

12 cm

4 cm

5 cm

Bend stakes at right angles.

After 4 rounds of A, insert additional stakes to right side of stakes.

Section A: Bend stakes at right angles. Work four rounds of three-rod wale.

Section B: Insert additional stakes and curve stakes outward to widen the edge into flare as shown. Work one round of three-rod wale 2.5 cm above the last round of section A.

Section C: Work four rounds of three-rod wale 3.5 cm above section B. Trim the end of one weaver. Work one round of pairing and trim remaining weavers.

The start of three-rod wale of section B and C.

①

②

③

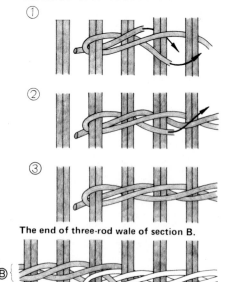

The end of three-rod wale of section B.

Ⓑ {

The finish of three-rod wale of section A.

Ⓐ {

How to weave 2nd round of section C.

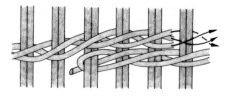

Basket with spiral design

shown on page 5

Two spirals are made on side of this basket. Take care not to deform the shape when you bend stakes. You may use the basket for a flower vase or a container.

FINISHED SIZE:

23 cm high and 20 cm in diameter across the top

EQUIPMENT AND MATERIALS:

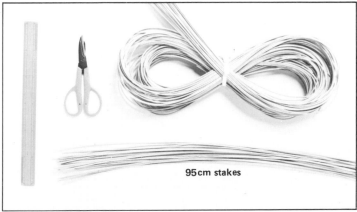

95 cm stakes

220 g of 2½ mm round rattan, cut into 25 stakes 95 cm long.

TECHNIQUES:

Woven base; Plain weave; Three-rod wale; Spiral design and Trac border C.

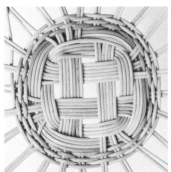

Base: Woven base

Side: Spiral design

Trac border C

DIRECTIONS:

1. Base

① Woven base

Start weaving.

7 stakes

6 stakes

6 stakes

6 stakes

4 rounds

10

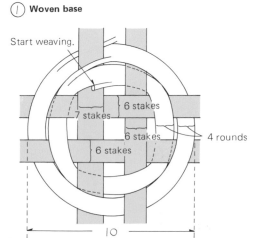

② Separate stakes into pairs.

Start weaving.

7 stakes   6 stakes

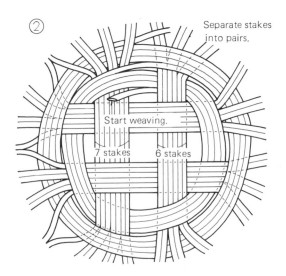

Make woven base as shown.
After eight rounds of plain weave, separate stakes into pairs. Weave to a diameter of 15 cm over pairs of stakes, followed by one round of three-rod wale.

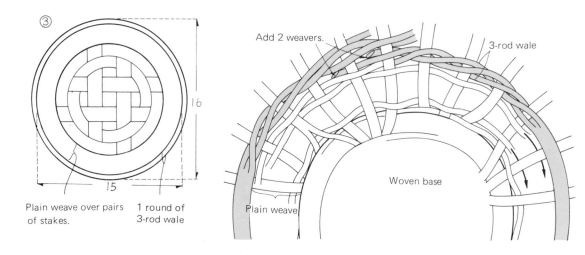

③

Plain weave over pairs of stakes.

1 round of 3-rod wale

Add 2 weavers.

3-rod wale

Woven base

Plain weave

2. Side

Turn over the base. Bend stakes at right angles.

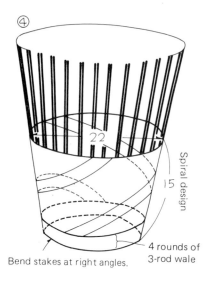

④

Bend stakes at right angles.

Spiral design

4 rounds of 3-rod wale

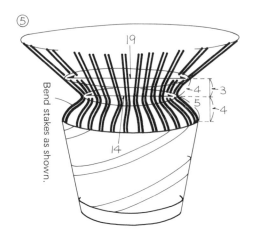

⑤

Bend stakes as shown.

After weaving 15 cm from the bottom, bend stakes inward with your fingers to achieve the tapered form at the neck as shown. Continue to weave in pattern, making spiral design to the top edge.

Spiral design

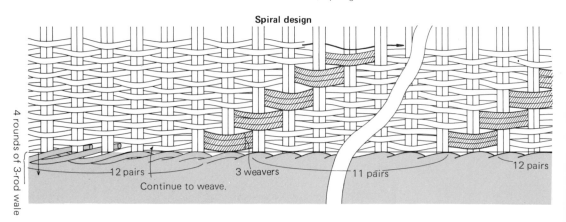

4 rounds of 3-rod wale

12 pairs

3 weavers

Continue to weave.

11 pairs

12 pairs

50

3. Border

Soak remaining stakes in water until pliable. Finish the edge with trac border C as shown.

Finished diagram

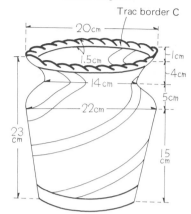

Trac border C

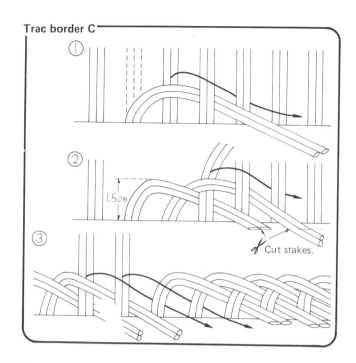

① ② ③

1.5cm

Cut stakes.

Striped basket

shown on page 12

The herringbone pattern is a variation of three-rod wale. This beautiful basket is made of brown and half-bleached round rattan. The shape is simple. Finish the edge with three rows of rolled border to make it strong.

FINISHED SIZE:

30cm high and 30cm in diameter across the top

EQUIPMENT AND MATERIALS:

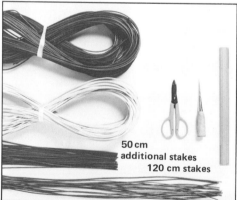

50 cm additional stakes
120 cm stakes

120 g of 2¾ mm half-bleached round rattan. 300 g of 2¾ mm brown round rattan, cut into 16 stakes 120 cm long and 32 additional stakes 50 cm long.

TECHNIQUES:

Woven base; Chasing;
Chain wale (Variation of three-rod wale);
Three-rod wale and
Rolled border.

Sides   Chain wale

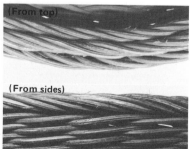

(From top)

(From sides)

Border   Rolled border (3 rows)

DIRECTIONS:
1. Base

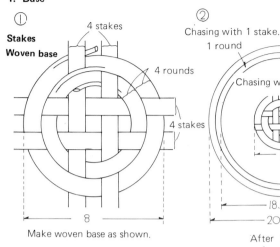

Stakes
Woven base

4 stakes
4 rounds
4 stakes
8

Make woven base as shown.

② Chasing with 1 stake.
1 round

Chasing with 2 stakes.

3-rod wale
1 round

8

18.5

20.5

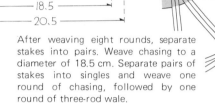

Add 1 weaver.
3-rod wale
Add 1 weaver.
1 stake
Chasing

After weaving eight rounds, separate stakes into pairs. Weave chasing to a diameter of 18.5 cm. Separate pairs of stakes into singles and weave one round of chasing, followed by one round of three-rod wale.

2. Side

Turn over the base. Bend stakes at right angles.

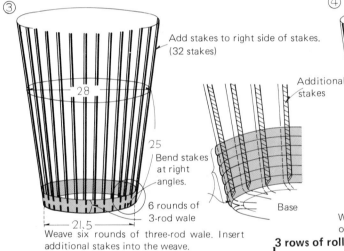

③ Add stakes to right side of stakes. (32 stakes)

28

Additional stakes

25
Bend stakes at right angles.

6 rounds of 3-rod wale

Base

21.5

Weave six rounds of three-rod wale. Insert additional stakes into the weave.

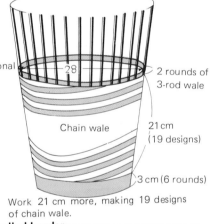

④ 28
2 rounds of 3-rod wale

Chain wale
21 cm (19 designs)

3 cm (6 rounds)

Work 21 cm more, making 19 designs of chain wale.

3. Border

Weave three rounds of three-rod wale, making an open space as shown. Soak remaining stakes in water until pliable. Finish the edge with three rows of rolled border.

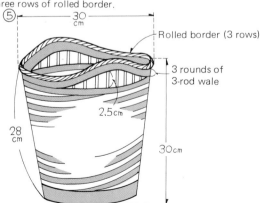

⑤ 30 cm

Rolled border (3 rows)

3 rounds of 3-rod wale

2.5 cm

28 cm

30 cm

3 rows of rolled border

1st row same as 1st row of page 36.

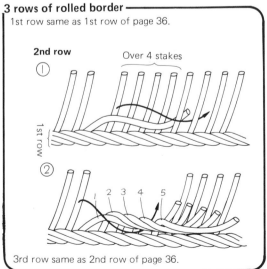

2nd row

① Over 4 stakes

1st row

② 1 2 3 4 5

3rd row same as 2nd row of page 36.

Chain wale

① Start weaving.

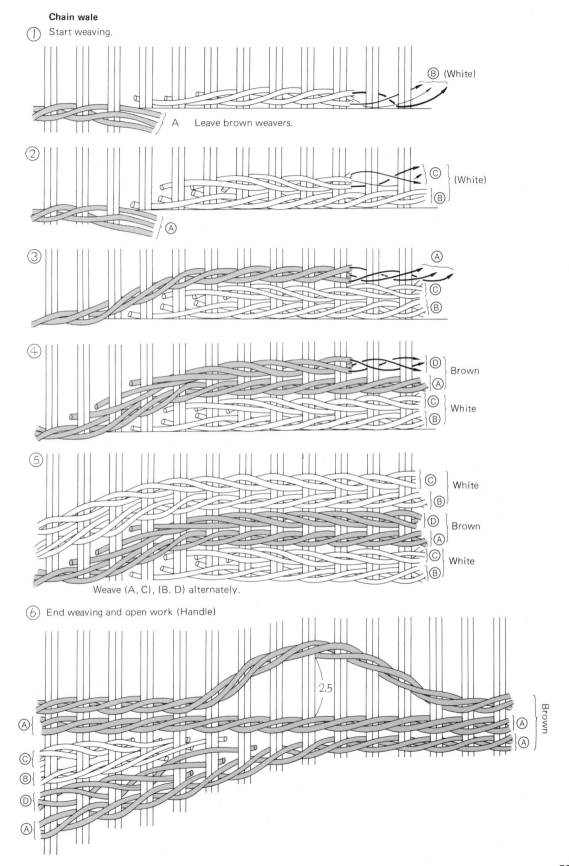

Ⓑ (White)

A   Leave brown weavers.

②

Ⓒ (White)
Ⓑ

Ⓐ

③

Ⓐ
Ⓒ
Ⓑ

④

Ⓓ Brown
Ⓐ
Ⓒ White
Ⓑ

⑤

Ⓒ White
Ⓑ
Ⓓ Brown
Ⓐ
Ⓒ White
Ⓑ

Weave (A, C), (B. D) alternately.

⑥ End weaving and open work (Handle)

2.5

Ⓐ
Ⓒ
Ⓑ
Ⓓ
Ⓐ

Ⓐ Brown
Ⓐ

Brown basket

shown on page 3
It does not take time to make the basket if you use plywood as a base. Line it with your favorite print and dye the rattan handle the same color as the basket.

FINISHED SIZE:

30.5 cm high including handle and 27 cm wide across the top.

TECHNIQUES:

Work with wooden base ... method B;
Three-rod wale; Plain weave and Trac border D.

EQUIPMENT AND MATERIALS:

32 cm additional stakes

50 cm stakes

10 mm round rattan

180 g of 3 mm brown round rattan, cut into 29 stakes 50 cm long and 29 additional stakes 32 cm long. 50 g of 5½ mm brown flat rattan. One length of 10 mm round rattan, 70 cm long. Plywood, 4.5 mm thick × 12 cm × 20 cm. Print for lining.

Side

Trac border D

DIRECTIONS:

1. Base

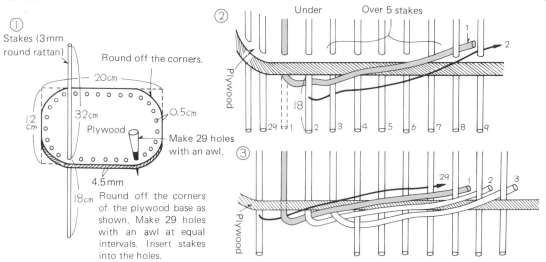

① Stakes (3mm round rattan)
Round off the corners.
20cm
32cm
12 cm
Plywood
0.5cm
Make 29 holes with an awl.
4.5 mm
18 cm Round off the corners of the plywood base as shown. Make 29 holes with an awl at equal intervals. Insert stakes into the holes.

② Under   Over 5 stakes
Plywood
18
29 1 2 3 4 5 6 7 8 9
1
2

③ Plywood
29 1 2 3

2. Side

Weave two rounds of three-rod wale using round rattan.

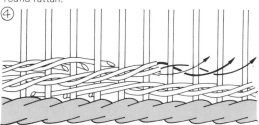

④

2 rounds of 3-rod wale

Bottom border

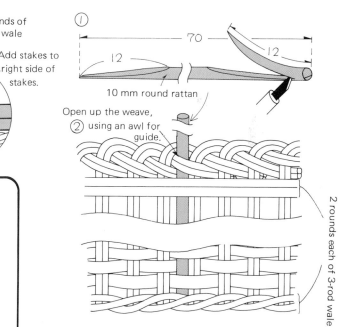

⑥

3-rod wale (3 mm round rattan)

11.5
Plain weave
Plain weave with uneven number of stakes.

Flat rattan

⑤

3-rod wale 2 rounds

14

11.5
Plain weave (flat rattan)

2 rounds of 3-rod wale

Bottom border

Add stakes to right side of stakes.

Insert additional stakes into the weave on the right side of each original stake. Weave with brown flat rattan as directed. When the weaver runs out, overlap ends of old and new weavers (see page 20). Weave two rounds of three-rod wale with round rattan.

4. Handle

Trim both ends of 10 mm round rattan on a diagonal and dye it in advance. Bend rattan into U-shape with trimmed ends inside.

①

70

12

12

10 mm round rattan

Open up the weave,
② using an awl for guide.

2 rounds each of 3-rod wale

3. Border

Finish the edge with trac border D as shown, using well-soaked stakes.

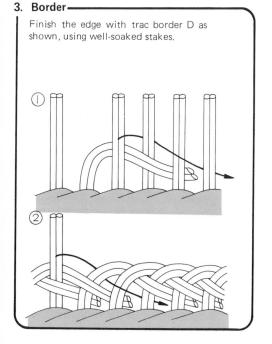

①

②

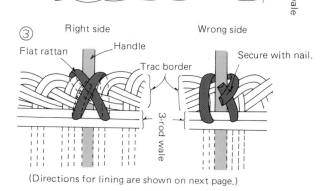

③

Right side

Flat rattan

Handle

Wrong side

Trac border

Secure with nail.

3-rod wale

(Directions for lining are shown on next page.)

5. Lining

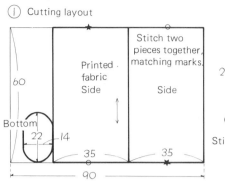

① Cutting layout

60

Printed fabric Side

Stitch two pieces together, matching marks.

Side

Bottom

22 — 14

35   35

90

Stitch two pieces together to make tube, matching marks.
Turn to the right side.
Run a gathering stitch at the bottom.
Fold 5 cm to the wrong side at the top.
Sew the base to the bottom of tube.

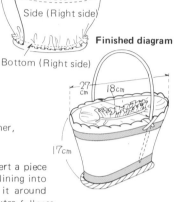

②

28 | 1

5

Margin

Gather

Seam   allowance
                1 cm

Stitch together.

Right side Bottom

Stitch two pieces together, matching marks.

③ Machine stitch 1 cm   Opening for elastic tape

3.5

Side (Right side)

Bottom (Right side)

Finished diagram

27 Cm   18cm

17cm

Stitch for casing. Insert a piece of elastic. Insert the lining into the basket and tack it around the edge, tucking in extra fullness.

Sewing basket with lid

shown on page 9
Pincushion fits in the concave of the lid. Line inside of the basket with matching print. Make the concave of the lid fit in the basket.

FINISHED SIZE:

16.5

16.5 cm high and 23 cm in diameter across the top

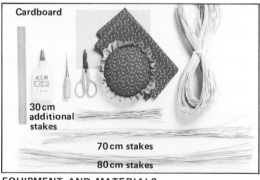

Cardboard

30cm additional stakes

70cm stakes

80cm stakes

EQUIPMENT AND MATERIALS:

300 g of 2 mm round rattan, cut into 24 stakes 80 cm long for basket, 16 stakes 70 cm long for lid and 32 additional stakes 30 cm long. Cotton print, 66 cm by 50 cm. Lace, 3 cm by 100 cm. Left-over yarn for stuffing. Cardboard.

TECHNIQUES:
Double cross base; Three-rod wale; Chasing and basic border A.

Double cross base

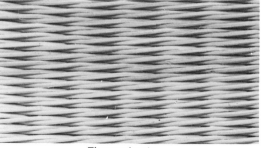

Three-rod wale

DIRECTIONS:

For basket:

1. Base

Double cross base

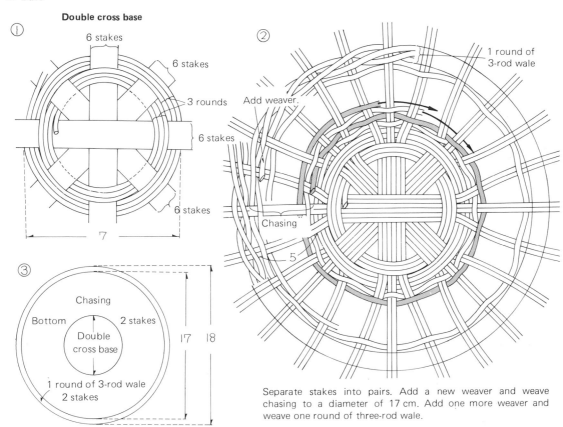

① 6 stakes
6 stakes
3 rounds
6 stakes
6 stakes
7

② 1 round of 3-rod wale
Add weaver.
Chasing
5

③ Chasing
Bottom   2 stakes
Double cross base
1 round of 3-rod wale
2 stakes
17 18

Separate stakes into pairs. Add a new weaver and weave chasing to a diameter of 17 cm. Add one more weaver and weave one round of three-rod wale.

2. Side

Turn over the base. Pat stakes close to the weave with sides of scissors. Bend stakes at right angles.

3. Border

Trim right-hand stakes as shown. Soak remaining stakes in water until pliable. Finish the edge with basic border A (see page 23).

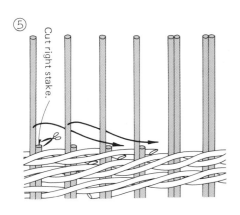

⑤ Cut right stake.

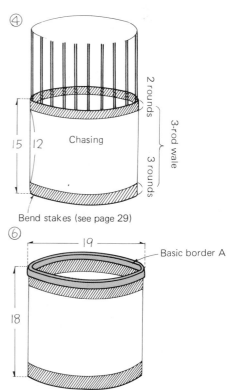

④ 2 rounds
3-rod wale
3 rounds
Chasing
15 12
Bend stakes (see page 29)

⑥ 19
Basic border A
18

For lid:

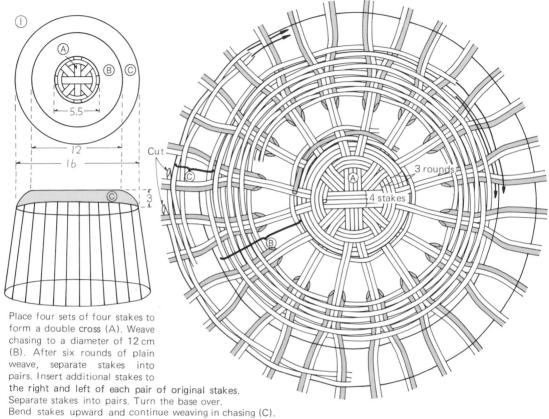

①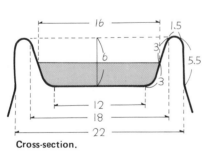

Place four sets of four stakes to form a double cross (A). Weave chasing to a diameter of 12 cm (B). After six rounds of plain weave, separate stakes into pairs. Insert additional stakes to the right and left of each pair of original stakes. Separate stakes into pairs. Turn the base over. Bend stakes upward and continue weaving in chasing (C).

Cross-section.

Bend stakes as shown.

③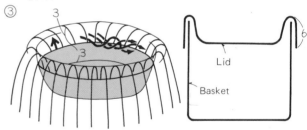

Add new weavers and weave three-rod wale in reverse direction.

④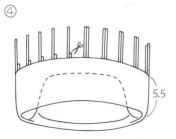

When the lid has reached 5.5 cm deep, trim right-hand stakes. Finish the lid with basic border A in the same manner as for the basket.

Finished diagram

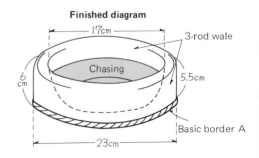

17cm

3-rod wale

Chasing

5.5cm

6 cm

Basic border A

23cm

For lining and pincushion:

Make lining a little bigger than the basket. Make pincushion to fit the concave of the lid.

① **Cutting layout**

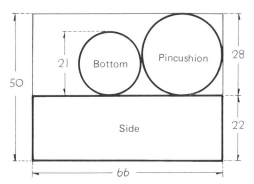

Place cardboard (17 cm in diameter) on the wrong side of lining for base as shown. Sew the base to side. Insert the lining into the basket and tack it around the edge.

② **Lining.**

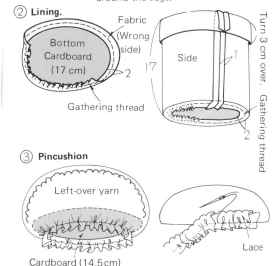

③ **Pincushion**

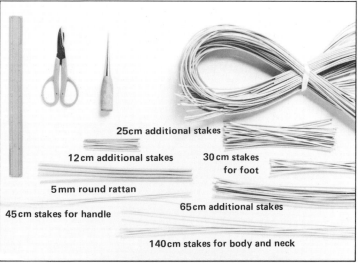

Flower vase with handles

shown on page 5

This basket does not need any special technique except shaping. Try to make perfect shape with great care.

FINISHED SIZE:

45 cm high and 35 cm wide including handles.

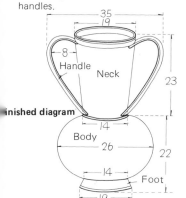

Finished diagram

EQUIPMENT AND MATERIALS:

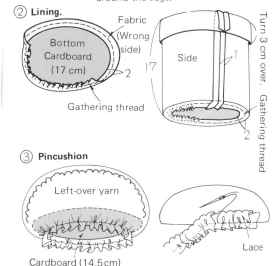

25cm additional stakes

12cm additional stakes

30 cm stakes for foot

5 mm round rattan

45cm stakes for handle

65cm additional stakes

140cm stakes for body and neck

500 g of 2¾ mm round rattan, cut into 9 stakes 140 cm long, 17 additional stakes 65 cm long and 34 additional stakes 25 cm long for neck and body, 17 stakes 30 cm long for foot, 4 stakes 45 cm long and 8 stakes 12 cm long for handles. 4 pieces of 5 mm round rattan, 32 cm long each.

TECHNIQUES:

Overlaid cross base; Under-two-over-two; Plain weave; Chasing; Pairing; Three-rod wale and Basic border A.

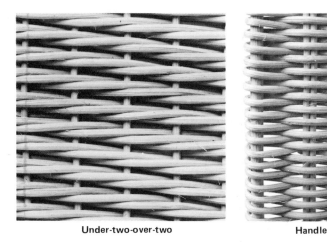

Under-two-over-two   **Handle**

DIRECTIONS:

1. Base

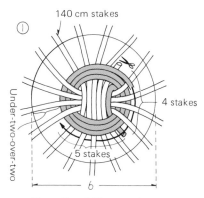

① 140 cm stakes

4 stakes

5 stakes

6

Under-two-over-two

Place five 140 cm stakes over four to form a cross.

② 140 cm stakes

65 cm additional stakes

2.5

Chasing (body)

Plain weave

14

Weave to a diameter of 14 cm and insert additional stakes into the weave.

2. Side

Turn over the base. Separate stakes into singles, evenly spaced.

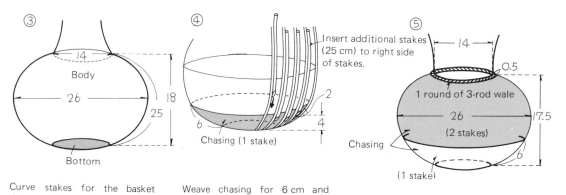

③

14

Body

26

18

25

Bottom

Curve stakes for the basket shape as shown.

④

Insert additional stakes (25 cm) to right side of stakes.

2

4

6

Chasing (1 stake)

Weave chasing for 6 cm and insert 25 cm stakes.

⑤

14

0.5

1 round of 3-rod wale

26

17.5

(2 stakes)

Chasing

6

(1 stake)

Continue to weave chasing over pairs of stakes.

3. Foot

Bend 30 cm stakes to U-shape and insert them into the edge of the base from inside.

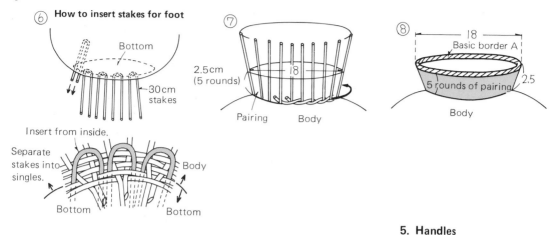

⑥ **How to insert stakes for foot**

Bottom

30 cm stakes

Insert from inside.

Separate stakes into singles.

Body

Bottom   Bottom

⑦ 2.5 cm (5 rounds)

18

Pairing   Body

⑧ 18

Basic border A

5 rounds of pairing   2.5

Body

5. Handles

Place two 45 cm stakes and two 5 mm round rattan as shown and weave 5 cm wide and 30 cm long, turning over at both sides. Trim both ends of two 5 mm round rattan and one center stake close to the weave. Insert 12 cm stakes as shown.

4. Neck

Trim one pair of stakes so that the number of stakes becomes uneven. Move stakes a little to adjust intervals between stakes.

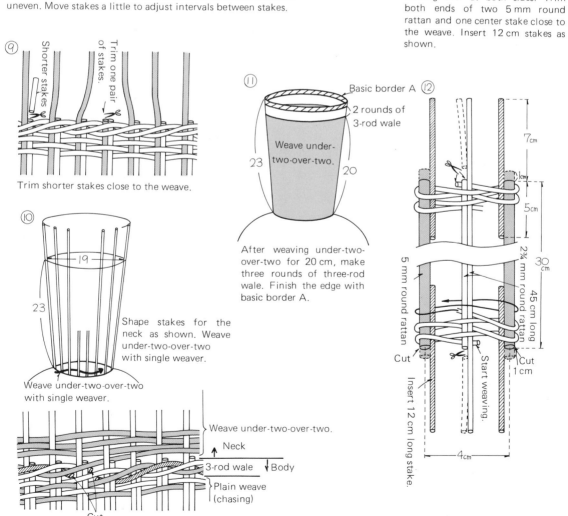

⑨ Shorter stakes

Trim one pair of stakes.

Trim shorter stakes close to the weave.

⑩ 19

23

Shape stakes for the neck as shown. Weave under-two-over-two with single weaver.

Weave under-two-over-two with single weaver.

Weave under-two-over-two.

Neck

3-rod wale ↓ Body

Plain weave (chasing)

Cut.

⑪ Basic border A

2 rounds of 3-rod wale

Weave under-two-over-two.

23   20

After weaving under-two-over-two for 20 cm, make three rounds of three-rod wale. Finish the edge with basic border A.

⑫ 7 cm

1 cm

5 cm

2¾ mm round rattan

30 cm

45 cm long

5 mm round rattan

Cut

Start weaving.

Cut 1 cm

Insert 12 cm long stake.

4 cm

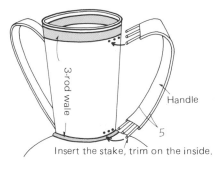

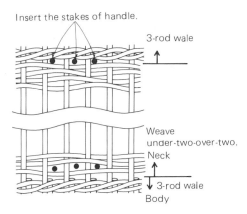

Insert the stakes of handle.

3-rod wale

Handle

3-rod wale

5

Insert the stake, trim on the inside.

Insert the stake ends of woven handles into top and bottom of the neck. Trim stakes on the inside after weaving (see page 24.).

Weave under-two-over-two.

Neck

3-rod wale
Body

All-purpose basket

shown on page 7

This is a useful basket — you can put anything in it. It also makes a good decoration for your room with its high back. Try to make angled corners.

FINISHED SIZE:

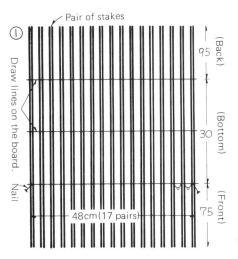

49

28

52

34

28 cm high x 52 cm wide x 34 cm long. The highest side (back), 49 cm high.

EQUIPMENT AND MATERIALS:

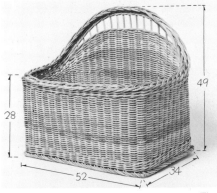

Board

3.5 mm

8 mm

1500 g of 3½ mm round rattan, cut into 34 stakes 200 cm long. 8 mm round rattan, one 180 cm length and 2 pieces each of 30 cm and 35 cm long.

TECHNIQUES:

Rectangular base; Chasing over pairs of stakes; Packing; Four-rod wale; Basic border B and Three-rod wale.

DIRECTIONS:

1. Base

Referring to page 31 for rectangular base, weave as directed. Draw 48 cm x 30 cm oblong and center lines in both directions on the board.

Place pairs of stakes on the board, evenly spaced.

① Pair of stakes

Draw lines on the board. Nail

(Back)
95

(Bottom)
30

(Front)
75

48cm(17 pairs)

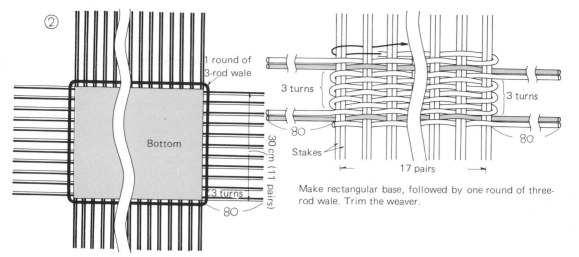

② 1 round of 3-rod wale

Bottom

3 turns

80

30 cm (11 pairs)

3 turns

3 turns

80

80

Stakes

17 pairs

Make rectangular base, followed by one round of three-rod wale. Trim the weaver.

2. Sides

Place 180 cm length of 8 mm round rattan around the base. Trim corners of rattan as shown to bend easily.

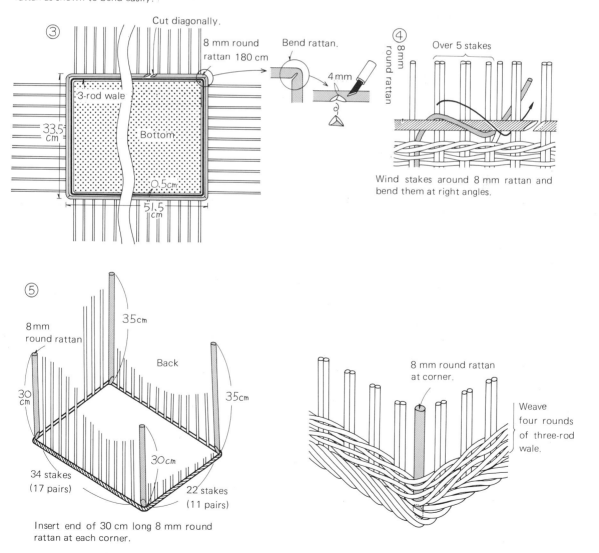

③ Cut diagonally.

8 mm round rattan 180 cm

3-rod wale

33.5 cm

Bottom

0.5 cm

51.5 cm

Bend rattan.

4 mm

④ 8 mm round rattan

Over 5 stakes

Wind stakes around 8 mm rattan and bend them at right angles.

⑤ 8 mm round rattan

35 cm

Back

35 cm

30 cm

30 cm

34 stakes (17 pairs)

22 stakes (11 pairs)

Insert end of 30 cm long 8 mm round rattan at each corner.

8 mm round rattan at corner.

Weave four rounds of three-rod wale.

3. Border

After weaving two rounds of four-rod wale, trim remaining ends of 8 mm rattan close to the weave. Soak remaining stakes in water until pliable. Finish the edge with basic border B (see page 40).

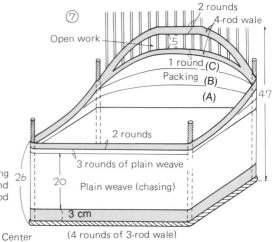

⑦

2 rounds
4-rod wale
Open work
1 round (C)
Packing (B)
(A)
47
2 rounds
3 rounds of plain weave
Plain weave (chasing)
3 cm
(4 rounds of 3-rod wale)
26
20

Trim one weaver and weave chasing for 20 cm. Weave packing for A, B and C of the back, followed by four-rod wale.

Packing of the back

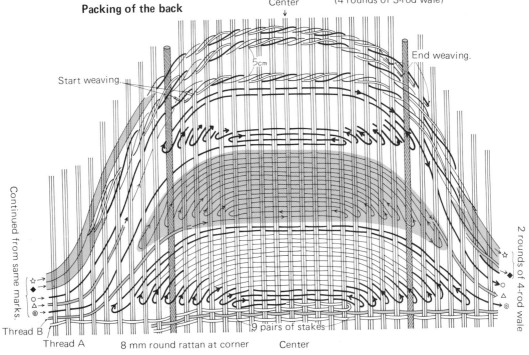

Center

Start weaving.

End weaving.

5 cm

Continued from same marks.

2 rounds of 4-rod wale

Thread B
Thread A
8 mm round rattan at corner
9 pairs of stakes
Center

Four-rod wale

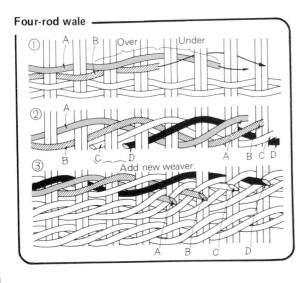

① A B Over Under
② A B C D A B C D
③ Add new weaver.
A B C D

Finished diagram

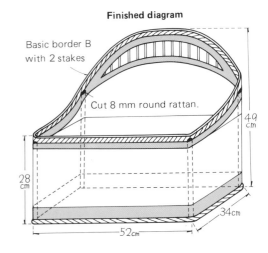

Basic border B with 2 stakes

Cut 8 mm round rattan.

49 cm

28 cm

34 cm

52 cm

64

Plant basket with cotton cord

shown on page 4

Three-rod wale is used for side. Dark and light green cotton cords are woven for an accent. Use cord in your favorite color.

FINISHED SIZE:

17.5 cm high and 23 cm in diameter across the top

EQUIPMENT AND MATERIALS:

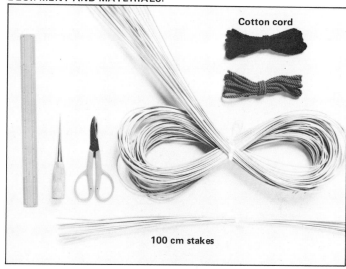

Cotton cord

100 cm stakes

TECHNIQUES:

Woven base; Chasing; Three-rod wale and Basic border A.

250g of 2½ mm round rattan, cut into 16 stakes 100 cm long. Cotton cord, dark and light green, 4.5 mm in diameter and 420 cm long each, cut into six 70 cm lengths.

DIRECTIONS:

1. Base

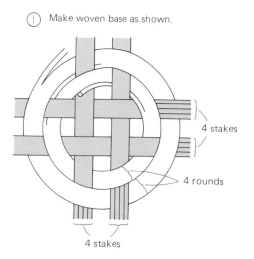

① Make woven base as shown.

4 stakes

4 rounds

4 stakes

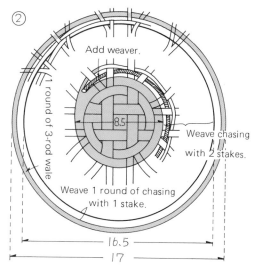

② Add weaver.

4 (1 round of 3-rod wale)

8.5

Weave chasing with 2 stakes.

Weave 1 round of chasing with 1 stake.

16.5

17

Separate stakes into pairs and weave chasing. Separate pairs of stakes into singles and weave one round of chasing. Add one more weaver and make a round of three-rod wale.

2. Side

Turn over the base.

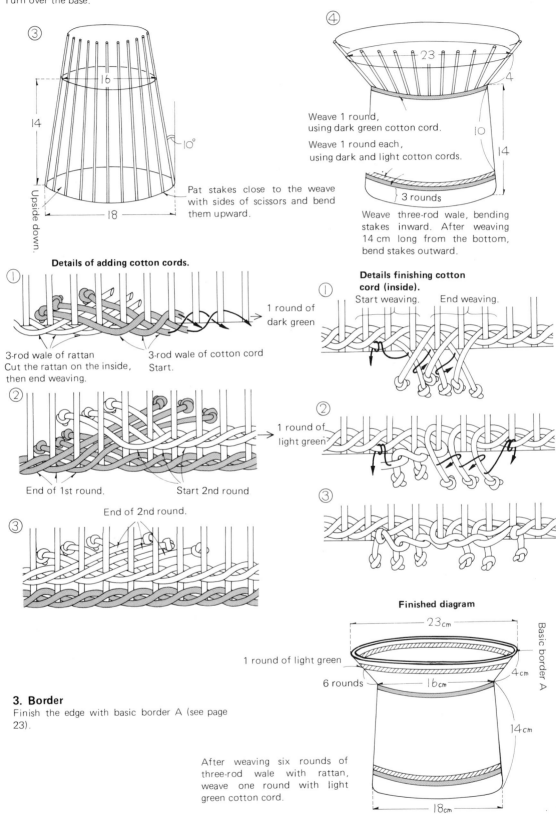

③

16

14

Upside down.

18

10°

Pat stakes close to the weave with sides of scissors and bend them upward.

④

23

4

10

14

Weave 1 round, using dark green cotton cord.

Weave 1 round each, using dark and light cotton cords.

3 rounds

Weave three-rod wale, bending stakes inward. After weaving 14 cm long from the bottom, bend stakes outward.

Details of adding cotton cords.

①

1 round of dark green

3-rod wale of rattan
Cut the rattan on the inside, then end weaving.

3-rod wale of cotton cord
Start.

②

1 round of light green

End of 1st round.

Start 2nd round

③

End of 2nd round.

Details finishing cotton cord (inside).

①

Start weaving.   End weaving.

②

③

Finished diagram

23cm

Basic border A

1 round of light green

6 rounds

16cm

4cm

14cm

18cm

3. Border

Finish the edge with basic border A (see page 23).

After weaving six rounds of three-rod wale with rattan, weave one round with light green cotton cord.

Plant basket with wooden beads

shown on page 4

Wooden beads are inserted into the openwork. Decide the width of the openwork based on the size of beads.

FINISHED SIZE:

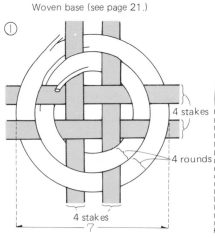

18 cm high and 27 cm in diameter across the top

Side, trac border E

EQUIPMENT AND MATERIALS:

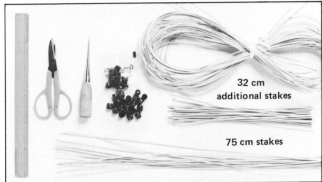

32 cm additional stakes

75 cm stakes

150g of 2 mm round rattan, cut into 16 stakes 75 cm long and 32 additional stakes 32 cm long. 32 brown wooden beads, 12 mm x 12 mm barrel shape.

TECHNIQUES:

Woven base; Chasing; Three-rod wale; Pairing and Trac border E.

DIRECTIONS:

1. Base

Woven base (see page 21.)

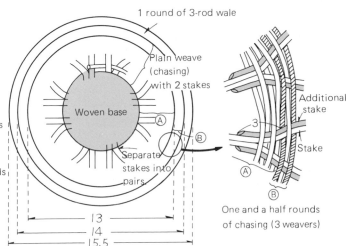

1 round of 3-rod wale

Plain weave (chasing) with 2 stakes

Woven base

(A)

(B)

Separate stakes into pairs.

4 stakes

4 rounds

4 stakes

7

13

14

15.5

Additional stake

3

Stake

(A)

(B)

One and a half rounds of chasing (3 weavers)

Separate stakes into pairs. Add another weaver and weave chasing (A). Insert additional stakes on the right and left sides of original stakes. Separate into pairs and weave one and a half rounds of chasing (B). Add third weaver and weave one round of three-rod wale.

2. Side

Turn over the base. Pat stakes close to the weave with sides of scissors. Bend stakes upward.

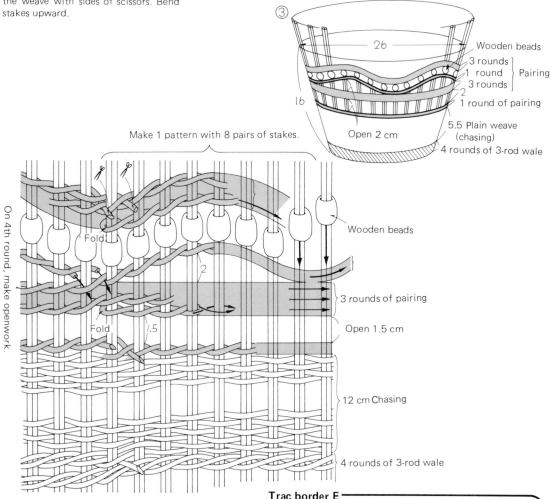

③

26

16

Wooden beads

3 rounds
1 round   } Pairing
3 rounds

1 round of pairing

Open 2 cm

5.5 Plain weave (chasing)

4 rounds of 3-rod wale

Make 1 pattern with 8 pairs of stakes.

On 4th round, make openwork.

Fold

Fold

2

1.5

Wooden beads

3 rounds of pairing

Open 1.5 cm

12 cm Chasing

4 rounds of 3-rod wale

3. Border

Soak remaining stakes in water until pliable. Finish the edge with trac border E. Trim stake ends on the inside, leaving about 1 cm.

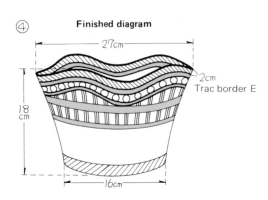

④ **Finished diagram**

27cm

2cm
Trac border E

18 cm

16cm

Trac border E

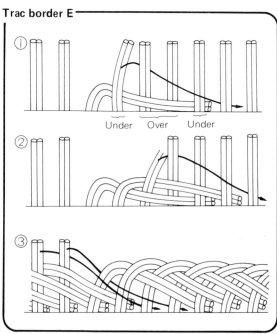

①

Under   Over   Under

②

③

Small basket with doll-shaped lid

shown on page 16

Wooden beads are used for head and body of the doll. This is a combination of two basic baskets. Make scarf and apron with your favorite print.

FINISHED SIZE:

22 cm tall and 16.5 cm in diameter across the bottom of the lid.

EQUIPMENT AND MATERIALS:

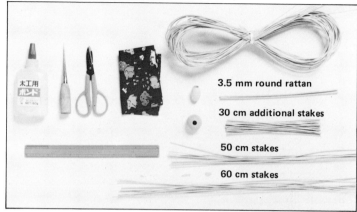

3.5 mm round rattan

30 cm additional stakes

50 cm stakes

60 cm stakes

150g of 2 mm round rattan, cut into 12 stakes 50 cm long and 24 additional stakes 30 cm long for body, 12 stakes 60 cm long and 24 additional stakes 30 cm long for lid. One length of 3½ mm round rattan, 26 cm long and two pieces of 11 cm long. Wooden beads in natural color, one round, 35 mm in diameter and one barrel shape, 21 mm x 32 mm. Cotton prints, 31 cm x 20 cm.

TECHNIQUES:

Overlaid cross base; Pairing; Chasing; Three-rod wale; Trac border B and Trac border D.

DIRECTIONS:
For body:
1. Base

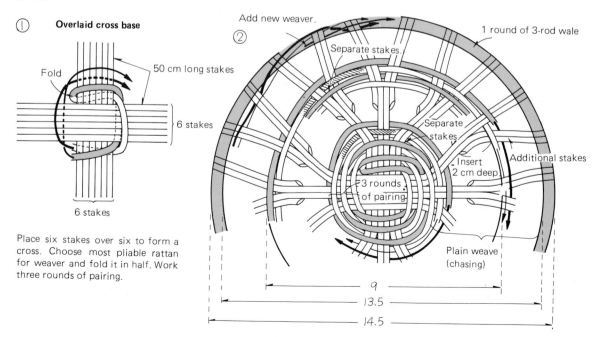

① **Overlaid cross base**

Fold

50 cm long stakes

6 stakes

6 stakes

Place six stakes over six to form a cross. Choose most pliable rattan for weaver and fold it in half. Work three rounds of pairing.

② Add new weaver.

Separate stakes.

1 round of 3-rod wale

Separate stakes

Insert 2 cm deep

Additional stakes

3 rounds of pairing

Plain weave (chasing)

9

13.5

14.5

2. Side

Turn over the base.

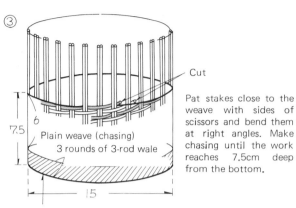

Pat stakes close to the weave with sides of scissors and bend them at right angles. Make chasing until the work reaches 7.5cm deep from the bottom.

Cut

7.5

6

Plain weave (chasing)
3 rounds of 3-rod wale

15

Pat stakes close to the weave with sides of scissors and bend them at right angles.

3. Border

Soak remaining stakes in water until pliable. Finish the edge with trac border D (see page 55).

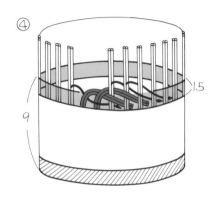

1.5

9

For cover (Doll's skirt):

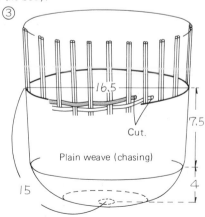

Leave weavers.

Separate stakes.

Insert.

Additional stakes

2

7.5

Chasing

Separate stakes into pairs.

11

Weave in the same manner as for the base of the body.

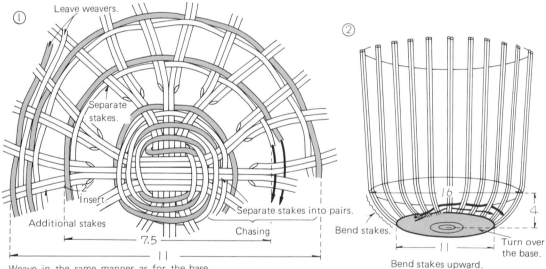

16

4

Bend stakes.

11

Turn over the base.

Bend stakes upward.

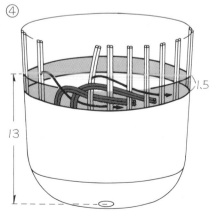

16.5

Cut.

Plain weave (chasing)

7.5

15

4

Weave chasing for 7.5 cm.

1.5

13

Soak remaining stakes in water. Finish the edge with trac border B (see page 47 for trac border B, but bend stakes in the reverse direction).

Finishing

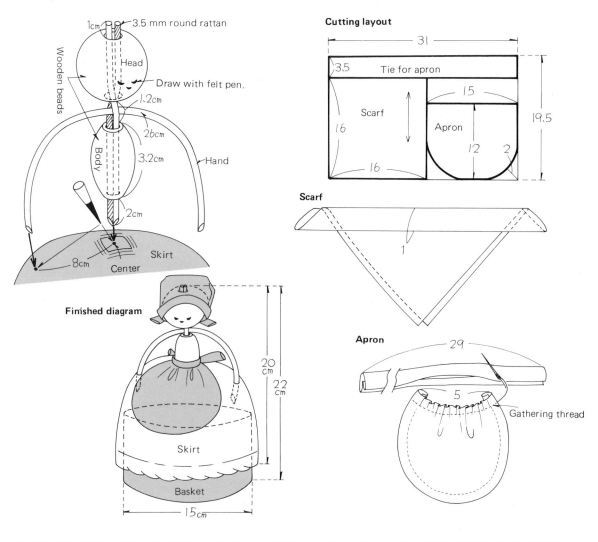

Head — 1cm — 3.5 mm round rattan

Wooden beads

Draw with felt pen.

1.2cm

26cm

Body — 3.2cm — Hand

2cm

8cm — Center — Skirt

Finished diagram

20 cm

22 cm

Skirt

Basket

15 cm

Cutting layout

31

3.5 — Tie for apron

Scarf — 15

16 — Apron — 12 — 2

16 — 19.5

Scarf

1

Apron

29

5

Gathering thread

Letter basket

shown on page 6

Add 7 mm round rattan for hanger to a basic rectangular basket. Insert Tyrolean tape or ribbon into the openwork.

FINISHED SIZE:

18

30

18 cm wide and 30 cm high including hanger

EQUIPMENT AND MATERIALS:

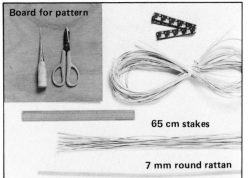

Board for pattern

65 cm stakes

7 mm round rattan

100g of 2 mm round rattan, cut into 20 stakes 65 cm long. 7 mm round rattan for hanger, 65 cm long. Tyrolean tape, 2 cm by 50 cm.

TECHNIQUES:

Rectangular base; Three-rod wale; Pairing and Basic border A (work with pairs of stakes).

DIRECTIONS:

1. Base

Draw 15.5 cm x 3.7 cm oblong on the board for pattern. Place pairs of stakes on the board, evenly spaced. Weave rectangular base referring to page 31.

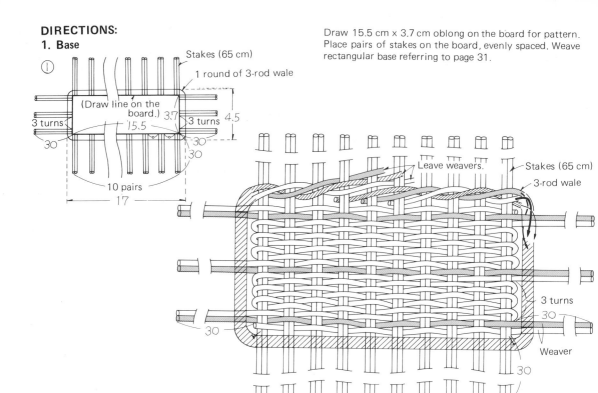

Stakes (65 cm)
1 round of 3-rod wale
(Draw line on the board.)
3.7
4.5
3 turns
15.5
3 turns
30
30
30
10 pairs
17

Leave weavers.
Stakes (65 cm)
3-rod wale
3 turns
30
Weaver
30
30

2. Sides

Turn over the base. Pat stakes close to the weave with sides of scissors and bend them upward. Weave sides as directed.

3. Border

Soak remaining stakes in water until pliable. Finish the edge with basic border A (see page 23), using pairs of stakes.

4. Hanger

Soak 7 mm round rattan in hot water until pliable. Bend well-soaked rattan as shown in the diagram. Attach hanger to the back of the basket with a pliable weaver.

5. Finishing

Shape and singe the fuzz. Insert Tyrolean tape into the open-work.

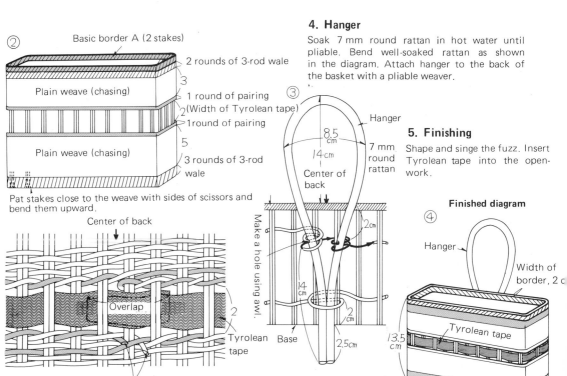

Basic border A (2 stakes)
2 rounds of 3-rod wale
3
Plain weave (chasing)
1 round of pairing
(Width of Tyrolean tape)
1 round of pairing
Plain weave (chasing)
5
3 rounds of 3-rod wale

Pat stakes close to the weave with sides of scissors and bend them upward.

Center of back
Overlap
2
Tyrolean tape
Cut the weaver.

Hanger
8.5 cm
14 cm
7 mm round rattan
Center of back
Make a hole using awl.
2 cm
4 cm
2 cm
Base
2.5 cm

Finished diagram

Hanger
Width of border, 2 c
Tyrolean tape
13.5 cm
18 cm
5.5 cm

Melon-shaped basket

shown on page 1

This unique basket is woven from one side to the other. You Min is used here, but it is hard for beginners to work with. Use 10 mm round rattan instead.

FINISHED SIZE

27

27 cm high including handle

EQUIPMENT AND MATERIALS:

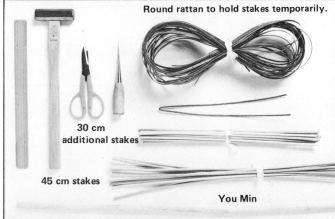

Round rattan to hold stakes temporarily.

30 cm additional stakes

45 cm stakes

You Min

Eye of God of four-fold bond

Border

200g of center-scraped peel of flat lapping rattan. 5 mm round rattan, 12 stakes 45 cm long and 12 additional stakes 30 cm long. 15 mm You Min, 2 stakes 83 cm long. 2½ mm round rattan, 60 cm long for holding stakes temporarily.

DIRECTIONS:
1. Frame

Bend You Min, after heating over a fire. When you use 10 mm round rattan, soak it in hot water until it bends easily. Make two circles 23 cm in diameter and form a cross. Nail the joint.

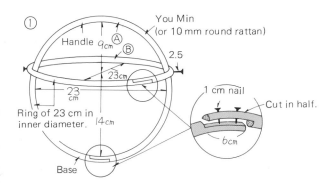

① Handle You Min (or 10 mm round rattan)
9 cm Ⓐ Ⓑ 2.5
23 cm
23 cm
Ring of 23 cm in inner diameter. 14 cm
1 cm nail
Cut in half.
6 cm
Base

2. Eye of God or Four-fold bond
Wrap where the frame crosses.
(Details are shown on next page.)

TECHNIQUES:
Eye of God or Four-fold bond and Plain weave.

Finished diagram

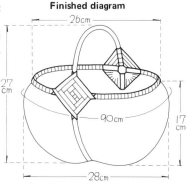

26 cm
27 cm
90 cm
17 cm
28 cm

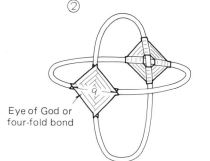

② Eye of God or four-fold bond

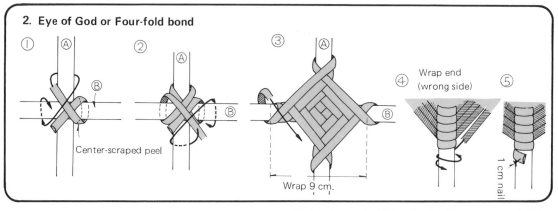

2. Eye of God or Four-fold bond

① A B — Center-scraped peel

② A B

③ A — Wrap 9 cm. B

④ Wrap end (wrong side)

⑤ 1 cm nail

3. Side and Base

Soak stakes and additional stakes in water to bend. Trim the ends of stakes on a diagonal and place six stakes on the back of Eye of God at quartered section. Work pairing with 2½ mm rattan to fix the stakes temporarily.

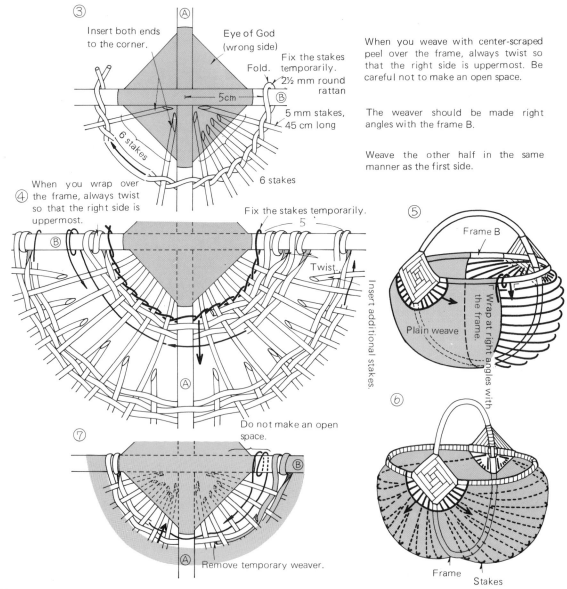

③ Insert both ends to the corner.

A

Eye of God (wrong side)

Fix the stakes temporarily.
Fold. 2½ mm round rattan

5cm — B

5 mm stakes, 45 cm long

6 stakes

6 stakes

④ When you wrap over the frame, always twist so that the right side is uppermost.

B

Fix the stakes temporarily.
5

Twist.

A

Insert additional stakes.

Do not make an open space.

⑦ Remove temporary weaver.

B

A

When you weave with center-scraped peel over the frame, always twist so that the right side is uppermost. Be careful not to make an open space.

The weaver should be made right angles with the frame B.

Weave the other half in the same manner as the first side.

⑤ Frame B

Plain weave

Wrap at right angles with the frame.

⑥ Frame — Stakes

Hen bread basket and chick egg stands

shown on page 10

This basket looks difficult to make, but make each part individually and assemble them together.

Hen

FINISHED SIZE:

25 cm high

EQUIPMENT AND MATERIALS:

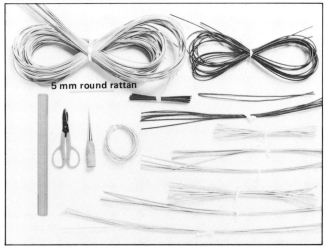

5 mm round rattan

200 g of 2½ mm round rattan, cut into 6 stakes 85 cm long, 8 stakes 80 cm long and 16 additional stakes 40 cm long for basket, 6 stakes 60 cm long, 8 stakes 50 cm long and 16 additional stakes 30 cm long for lid. 30 g of 2½ mm brown round rattan, cut into 6 stakes 60 cm long and 11 additional stakes 15 cm long for head, and 2 stakes 30 cm long for tail. 10 g of 1¾ mm round rattan, cut into 5 stakes 12 cm long for crest. 10 cm length of 5 mm round rattan.

TECHNIQUES:

Oval base A; Overlaid cross base; Chasing; Plain weave; Packing; Three-rod wale; Basic border A and Trac border D.

DIRECTIONS:
For basket (body):

1. Base
Weave a basic oval basket.

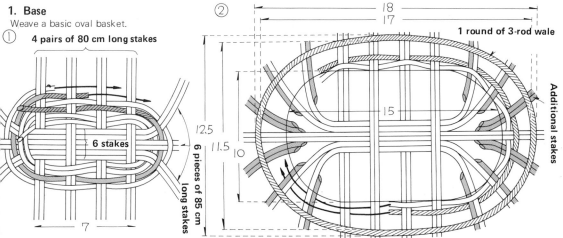

① 4 pairs of 80 cm long stakes

6 stakes

7

② 18 / 17

1 round of 3-rod wale

Additional stakes

12.5 / 11.5 10

6 pieces of 85 cm long stakes

15

Place stakes as shown. Weave two rounds of plain weave with a pliable weaver. Add another weaver and separate longer stakes into pairs. Weave chasing over pairs of stakes.

After weaving to 15 cm wide at the widest part, insert additional stakes. Continue to weave to 17 cm wide over pairs of stakes, followed by one round of three-rod wale.

2. Side

Turn over the base. Pat stakes close to the weave with sides of scissors and bend them upward.

3. Border

Soak remaining stakes in water until pliable. Finish the edge with basic border A (see page 23).

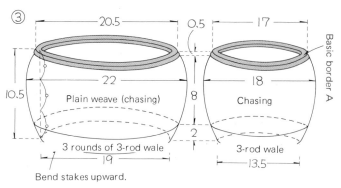

③

20.5   0.5   17

22   8   18

10.5   Plain weave (chasing)   Chasing

2

3 rounds of 3-rod wale   3-rod wale

19   13.5

Bend stakes upward.

Weave three rounds of three-rod wale. Trim one of the weavers and weave chasing to the edge.

Basic border A

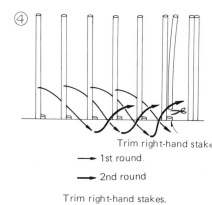

④

Trim right-hand stakes

→ 1st round.

→ 2nd round.

Trim right-hand stakes.

For lid:

Make the lid to fit the basket.

1. Base

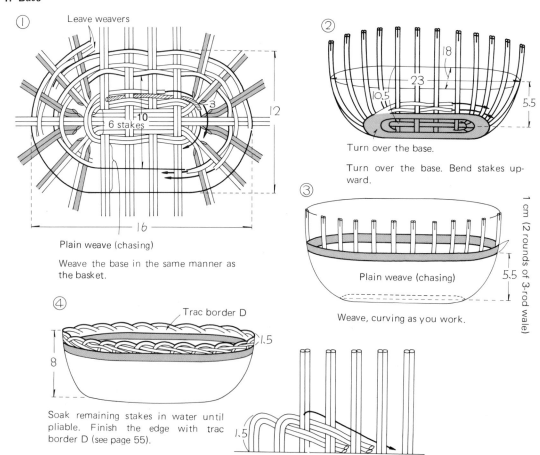

① Leave weavers

10
6 stakes   3   12

16

Plain weave (chasing)

Weave the base in the same manner as the basket.

②

18

23

10.5   5.5

Turn over the base.

Turn over the base. Bend stakes upward.

③

Plain weave (chasing)

5.5

1 cm (2 rounds of 3-rod wale)

Weave, curving as you work.

④ Trac border D

1.5

8

Soak remaining stakes in water until pliable. Finish the edge with trac border D (see page 55).

1.5

2. Head

Use brown round rattan.

①

Overlaid cross base

6
1
Packing
Plain weave
10
3.5
5.5
2.5
Packing
2.5
1.5
1.5
Finish with the trac border D.
11
9.5

②

Trim 1 stake.

Make a cross base with six stakes.
Weave packing to form head.

③ **Packing for section D.**

9.5

8.5

Weave packing for section D, to fit the top of the lid.

Border

④

Additional stakes

9.5

8.5

Insert additional stakes and finish the edge with trac border D.

Additional stakes

3. Tail and crest

Use brown rattan for tail and half-bleached rattan for crest.

① **Tail**

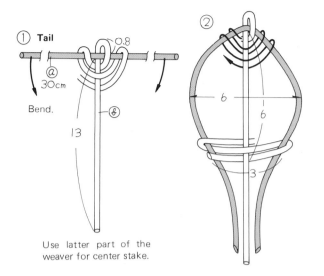

0.8

ⓐ
30cm

Bend.

13

ⓑ

Use latter part of the weaver for center stake.

②

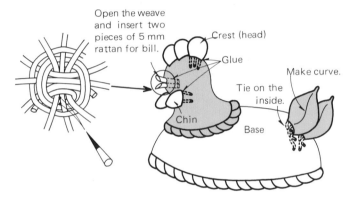

6

6

3

Crest (head) Make 3 pieces.

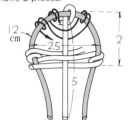

12 cm

2.5

2

5

Crest (chin) Make 2 pieces.

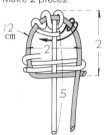

12 cm

2

2

5

4. Assemble

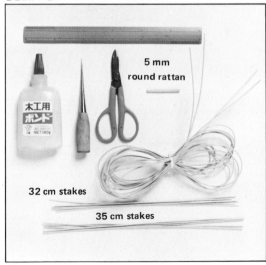

Open the weave and insert two pieces of 5 mm rattan for bill.

Crest (head)

Glue

Make curve.

Tie on the inside.

Chin

Base

For chicks:

FINISHED SIZE:

7.5

7.5 cm high

TECHNIQUES:

Overlaid cross base; Under-two-over-two; Plain weave; Three-rod wale; Packing and Basic border A.

EQUIPMENT AND MATERIALS:

5 mm round rattan

木工用
ボンド
NET 180g

32 cm stakes

35 cm stakes

25 g of 2 mm round rattan, cut into 6 stakes 35 cm long for body and 6 stakes 32 cm long for head. 4 cm length of 5 mm round rattan.

DIRECTIONS:

1. Head

Make Overlaid cross base.

Turn over the base. Bend stakes upward.
Insert two pieces of 5 mm rattan for bill. Finish the edge with basic border A.

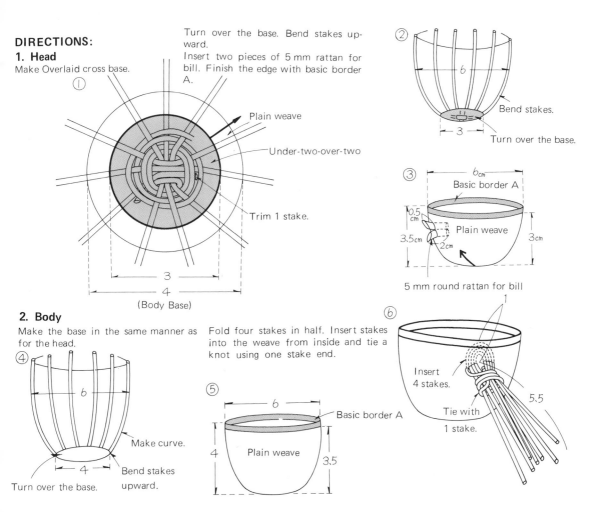

① Plain weave

Under-two-over-two

Trim 1 stake.

3

4

(Body Base)

② Bend stakes.

6

3

Turn over the base.

③ 6cm

Basic border A

0.5 cm

3.5 cm

2 cm

Plain weave

3 cm

5 mm round rattan for bill

2. Body

Make the base in the same manner as for the head.

Fold four stakes in half. Insert stakes into the weave from inside and tie a knot using one stake end.

④ 6

Make curve.

Turn over the base.

Bend stakes upward.

4

⑤ 6

Basic border A

4 Plain weave 3.5

⑥ 1

Insert 4 stakes.

Tie with 1 stake.

5.5

Donkey

shown on page 14

Make head, body and legs individually. Then assemble them together. Weave in the same manner as for making small baskets. Tyrolean tape is used for saddlecloth. Use print desired.

FINISHED SIZE:

32.5

32.5 cm high

EQUIPMENT AND MATERIALS:

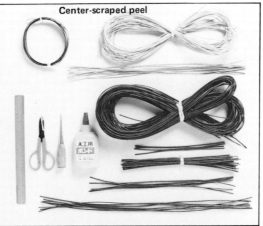

Center-scraped peel

木工用

200 g of 2½ mm brown round rattan, cut into 8 stakes 65 cm long for body, 24 stakes 35 cm long for legs, 7 stakes 40 cm long for head and 4 stakes 25 cm long for ears. 3 m length of center-scraped peel of flat lapping rattan. 50 g of 2 mm round rattan for two baskets, cut into 14 stakes 50 cm long. Two pieces of 3½ mm round rattan, 16 cm long. 2 mm center-scraped peel, 30 cm long. Marbles for weight. Wire. Tyrolean tape, 5.5 cm by 2.5 cm. Cord.

DIRECTIONS:

1. Body

Weave from the back of the body to the neck. Weave under body and neck, packing as shown.

TECHNIQUES:

Overlaid cross base; Under-two-over-two; Plain weave; Three-rod wale; Packing and Basic border A,

Place four stakes over four to form a cross (see page 25). Weave to a diameter of 4.5 cm and turn over the base. Weave body, curving stakes. Weave packing for chest. Weave to the neck.

5 — 11 stakes

11

2.5

Neck
Plain weave

Leave 3-4 cm.

Packing

7.5

1

②

Center of abdomen

Center of back

Body

Plain weave
(15 stakes)

11.5

1.5

Make curve.

Turn over the base.

Plain weave

Trim 1 stake.

Under-two-over-two

4.5

8.5

Center of back   Center of abdomen   Center of back

B

A

Packing

2.5   1

6 5 4 3 2 1   1 2 3 4 5 6

80

2. Head

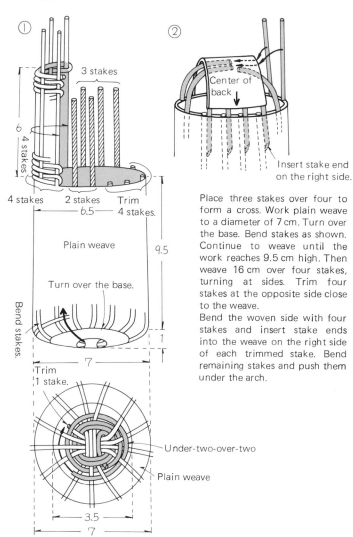

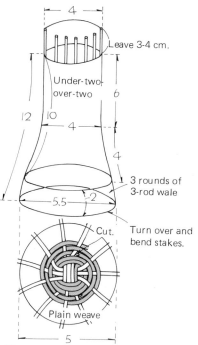

Insert stake end on the right side.

Place three stakes over four to form a cross. Work plain weave to a diameter of 7 cm. Turn over the base. Bend stakes as shown. Continue to weave until the work reaches 9.5 cm high. Then weave 16 cm over four stakes, turning at sides. Trim four stakes at the opposite side close to the weave.

Bend the woven side with four stakes and insert stake ends into the weave on the right side of each trimmed stake. Bend remaining stakes and push them under the arch.

3. Legs

Place three stakes over three to form a cross. Weave to a diameter of 5 cm and turn over. Shape stakes for leg. Add two more weavers and make three rounds of three-rod wale. Trim two weavers. Weave under-two-over-two (see page 25) for 10 cm.

4. Ears

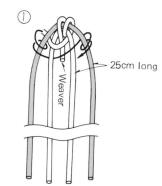

Bend two stakes to form U-shape.

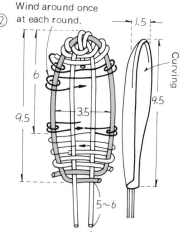

Weave as shown wrapping around side stakes and curving.

5. Mane and tail

Soak materials for mane and tail in water until pliable.

Mane:

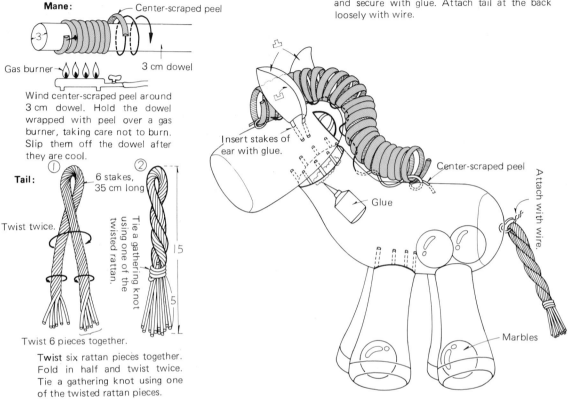

Center-scraped peel

Gas burner

3 cm dowel

Wind center-scraped peel around 3 cm dowel. Hold the dowel wrapped with peel over a gas burner, taking care not to burn. Slip them off the dowel after they are cool.

Tail:

① 6 stakes, 35 cm long

Twist twice.

Twist 6 pieces together.

② Tie a gathering knot using one of the twisted rattan.

15

5

Twist six rattan pieces together. Fold in half and twist twice. Tie a gathering knot using one of the twisted rattan pieces.

6. Assemble

Place marbles or small stones for a weight into legs and body. Insert stakes of the leg into body, neck stakes into head and attach mane along head and neck. Insert ear stakes into head and secure with glue. Attach tail at the back loosely with wire.

Insert stakes of ear with glue.

Center-scraped peel

Attach with wire.

Glue

Marbles

7. Baskets

Make two tiny baskets with 2 mm rattan. Tie two baskets with cord.

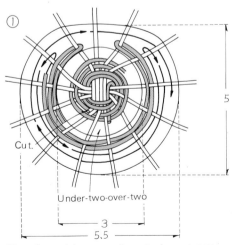

①

5

Cut.

Under-two-over-two

3

5.5

Place four stakes over three to form a cross. Weave and pack as shown.

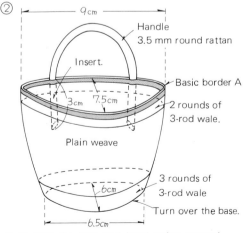

②

9 cm

Handle 3.5 mm round rattan

Insert.

3cm 7.5cm

Basic border A

2 rounds of 3-rod wale.

Plain weave

3 rounds of 3-rod wale

6cm

Turn over the base.

6.5cm

Turn over the base and bend stakes upward. Work three rounds of three-rod wale. Weave under-one-over-one. After two rounds of three-rod wale, finish the basket with basic border A. Insert 3.5 mm rattan into the weave for handle.

Freight train

shown on page 15

You can change small baskets into freight train by attaching wooden rings. Use of the train for a penstand, or as a container for small things and candies. Practice making rectangular base with single stakes.

Locomotive

FINISHED SIZE:

14

10   15

EQUIPMENT AND MATERIALS:

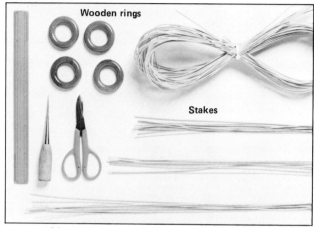

Wooden rings

Stakes

130 g of 2 mm round rattan, cut into 10 stakes 35 cm long, 7 stakes 45 cm long and 8 stakes 60 cm long. Four brown wooden rings, 5.5 cm in diameter. Board for pattern.

TECHNIQUES:
Rectangular base with single stakes; Overlaid cross base; Under-two-over-two; Plain weave; Three-rod wale and Basic border A.

DIRECTIONS:
1. Base

Draw 13 cm x 7 cm oblong on the board and place ten 35 cm stakes at equal intervals.

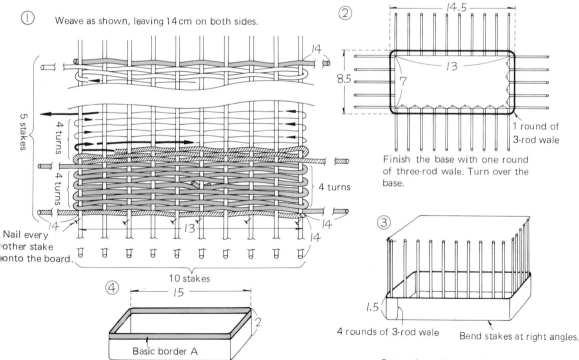

① Weave as shown, leaving 14 cm on both sides.

14

5 stakes

4 turns

4 turns

4 turns

14   13   14
14

Nail every other stake onto the board.

10 stakes

② 14.5

13

8.5   7

1 round of 3-rod wale

Finish the base with one round of three-rod wale. Turn over the base.

③

1.5

4 rounds of 3-rod wale   Bend stakes at right angles.

Pat stakes close to the weave with sides of scissors. Bend stakes at right angles, followed by four rounds of three-rod wale.

④ ⊢ 15 ⊣

2

Basic border A

Soak stakes in water until pliable and finish with basic border A (see page 23).

83

2. Small chimney

Form a cross with four 45 cm stakes and three stakes of the same length.

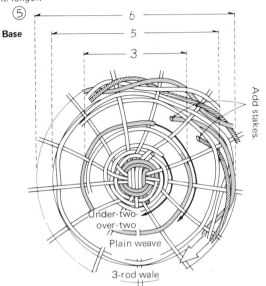

⑤ **Base**

6
5
3

Add stakes.

Under-two-over-two

Plain weave

3-rod wale

Weave to a diameter of 6 cm. Turn over the base.

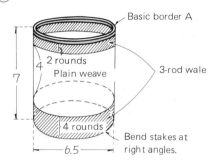

⑥ **Side**

Basic border A

2 rounds
4 Plain weave
7
3-rod wale

4 rounds

6.5

Bend stakes at right angles.

Bend stakes at right angles. Weave as directed in the diagram. Soak remaining stakes in water. Finish the edge with basic border A.

3. Large chimney

Form a cross with two sets of four 60 cm stakes.

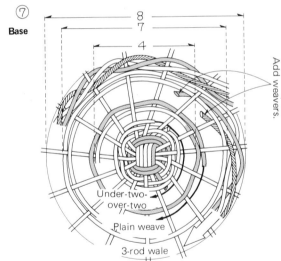

⑦ **Base**

8
7
4

Add weavers.

Under-two-over-two

Plain weave

3-rod wale

Weave as directed to a diameter of 8 cm. Turn over the base.

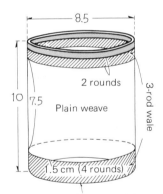

⑧ **Side**

8.5

2 rounds
10 7.5
Plain weave
3-rod wale

1.5 cm (4 rounds)

Bend stakes at right angles.

Make sides in the same manner as the small chimney.

4. Assemble

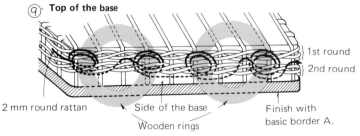

⑨ **Top of the base**

1st round
2nd round

2 mm round rattan   Side of the base   Finish with basic border A.

Wooden rings

Attach wooden rings to each side of the base.

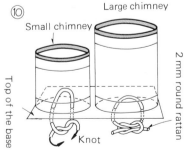

⑩

Large chimney

Small chimney

Top of the base

2 mm round rattan

Knot

Attach small and large chimneys to the top of the base.

Freight train A

FINISHED SIZE:

10.5 cm wide x 14 cm long x 10 cm high

TECHNIQUES:

Rectangular base; Three-rod wale; Chasing and Basic border A and Packing.

EQUIPMENT AND MATERIALS:

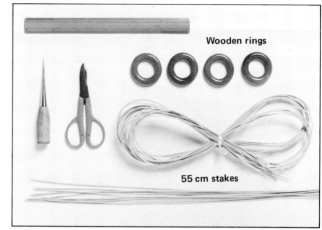

Wooden rings

55 cm stakes

100 g of 2 mm round rattan, cut into 9 stakes 55 cm long. Four brown wooden rings, 5.5 cm in diameter. Board for pattern.

DIRECTIONS:

Draw 11.5 cm x 7 cm oblong on the board. Place stakes on the board at equal intervals.

1. Base

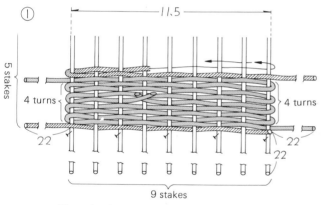

Weave in the same manner as the locomotive base.

2. Sides

Turn over the base. Bend stakes at right angles.

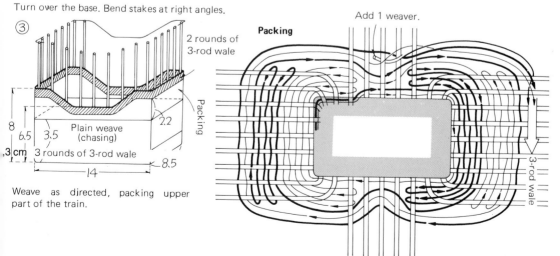

Weave as directed, packing upper part of the train.

3. Border

Soak remaining stakes in water. Finish the train with basic border A (see page 23).

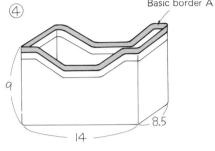

Basic border A

④

9

14

8.5

4. Wheels

Attach wooden rings in place with well-soaked rattan.

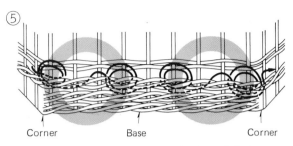

⑤

Corner   Base   Corner

Thread a weaver between three-rod wale and chasing to fix rings.

Freight train B

FINISHED SIZE:

10

10.5   14

10.5 cm wide x 14 cm long x 10 cm high

TECHNIQUES:

Rectangular base with single stakes; Three-rod wale; Chasing and Basic border A.

EQUIPMENT AND MATERIALS:

Wooden rings

40 cm stakes for roof

55 cm stakes for body

120 g of 2 mm round rattan, cut into 9 stakes 55 cm long for body and 9 stakes 40 cm long for roof. Board for pattern. Four brown wooden rings, 5.5 cm in diameter.

DIRECTIONS:

1. Body

Make base in the same manner as freight train A. Weave 9 cm to make a rectangular body.

2. Roof

Draw 11.5 cm x 9 cm oblong on the board. Place stakes on the board at equal intervals. Make roof in the same manner as the base of freight train A. Weave until there are six stakes at each side. Work one round of three-rod wale. Soak remaining stakes in water and finish the edge with basic border A.

Basic border A
2 rounds
Plain weave (chasing)
6
3-rod wale
14
9
11.5
7 Base
Rectangular base
8.5
3 rounds
1 round of 3-rod wale

Bend stakes at right angles.

①
15
13.5
11.5
4 turns
2 rounds of 3-rod wale
Basic border A
6 stakes
10.5
9
11.5
Roof
4 turns
15
15
9 stakes

Tie with a cord.

②

8.5

Wet the finished work and shape as shown. Tie the shaped roof with a cord until dry.

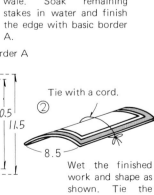

3. Assemble

Attach wooden rings in place. Attach the roof to the body loosely with pliable so that it opens easily. Tie ends of rattan on the inside.

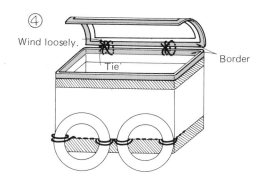

Wind loosely.

Tie

Border

---

shown on page 16

Two mirror frames

You can make any size mirror frame by changing the thickness of rattan and/or number of stakes according to the size of a mirror. Make the frame to fit the mirror exactly.

FINISHED SIZE:

34

34 cm wide including handles

EQUIPMENT AND MATERIALS:

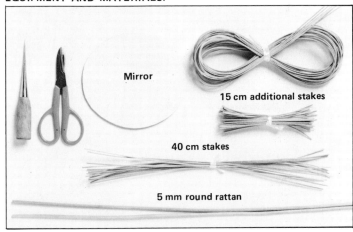

Mirror

15 cm additional stakes

40 cm stakes

5 mm round rattan

50 g of 1¾ mm round rattan, cut into 16 stakes 40 cm long and 64 additional stakes 15 cm long. Two pieces of 5 mm round rattan, 85 cm long. Mirror, 15.5 cm x 13.5 cm oval.

TECHNIQUES:

Woven base; Spiral pairing; Chasing and Decorative border.

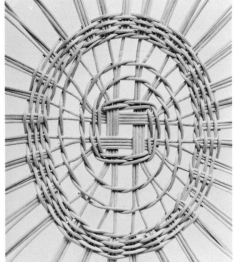

Wrong side (woven base, spiral pairing)

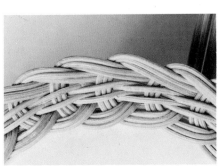

Decorative border

DIRECTIONS:
1. Background

Make background, according to the shape and size of mirror.

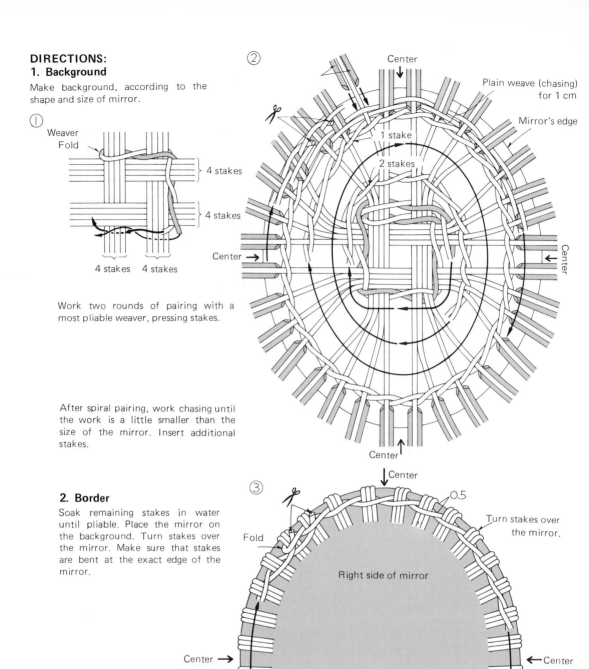

① Weaver
Fold

} 4 stakes

} 4 stakes

4 stakes 4 stakes

Work two rounds of pairing with a most pliable weaver, pressing stakes.

After spiral pairing, work chasing until the work is a little smaller than the size of the mirror. Insert additional stakes.

② Center

Plain weave (chasing) for 1 cm

Mirror's edge

1 stake

2 stakes

Center →

← Center

Center →

Center ↑

2. Border

Soak remaining stakes in water until pliable. Place the mirror on the background. Turn stakes over the mirror. Make sure that stakes are bent at the exact edge of the mirror.

③ ↓ Center

0.5

Turn stakes over the mirror.

Fold

Right side of mirror

Center →

← Center

Work one round of pairing, to fix the stakes and the mirror.

④

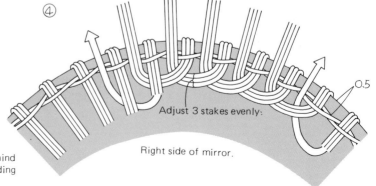

Adjust 3 stakes evenly.

0.5

Right side of mirror.

Take each group of stakes behind the next all the way round, bending upward as shown.

88

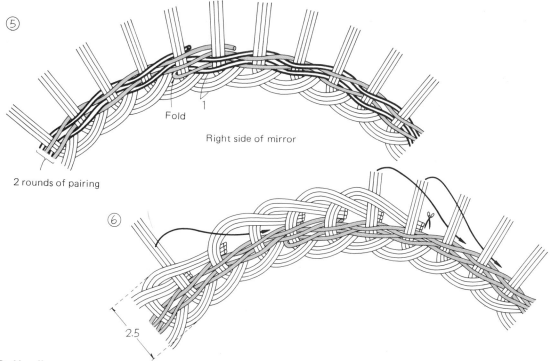

⑤

Fold

1

Right side of mirror

2 rounds of pairing

⑥

2.5

3. Handle

Soak 5 mm rattan in water until pliable. Fold soaked-rattan as shown in the diagram (7). Wrap the center of the handle, using a pliable weaver.

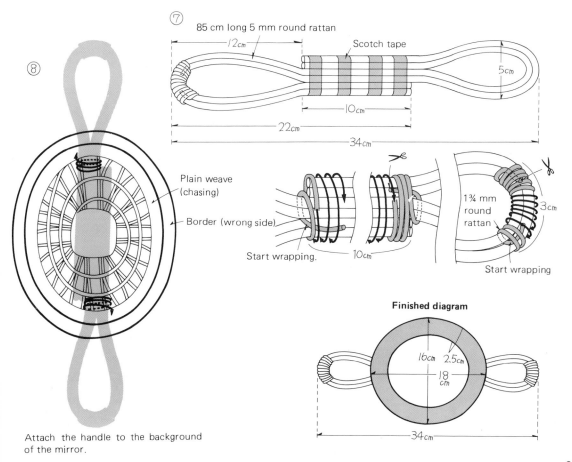

⑦ 85 cm long 5 mm round rattan

12cm

Scotch tape

5cm

22cm

10cm

34cm

⑧

Plain weave (chasing)

Border (wrong side)

Start wrapping.

10cm

1¾ mm round rattan

3cm

Start wrapping

Attach the handle to the background of the mirror.

Finished diagram

16cm 2.5cm

18 cm

34cm

Small mirror frame
FINISHED SIZE:

8.5 cm in diameter

MATERIALS:

20 g of 1½ mm round rattan, cut into 10 stakes 30 cm long and 19 additional stakes 10 cm long. 5 mm round rattan, 28 cm long. Round mirror, 7 cm in diameter.

DIRECTIONS:

Place five stakes over five to form a cross. Weave according to the size of the mirror. Insert additional stakes on the right side of each original stake. Finish the frame with decorative border in the same manner as the oval mirror frame.

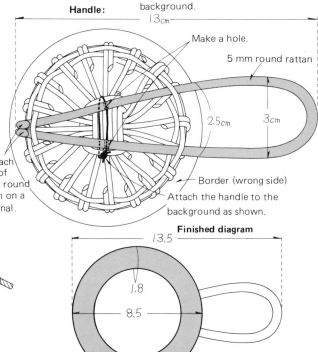

Bend as shown and attach to the background.

Handle: 13cm

Make a hole.

5 mm round rattan

2.5 cm · 3 cm

Border (wrong side)

Attach the handle to the background as shown.

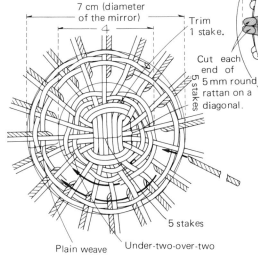

7 cm (diameter of the mirror) · 4

Trim 1 stake.

5 stakes

Cut each end of 5 mm round rattan on a diagonal.

5 stakes

Plain weave · Under-two-over-two

Finished diagram

13.5

1.8

8.5

Decorative border with 2 stakes

Doll-shaped flower vase

shown on page 13

This is a basic round basket with stand in the guise of a doll. Attach large and small leaves for hair, covering front and back of head. Arrange flowers like a crown.

FINISHED SIZE:

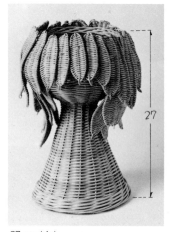

27 cm high

EQUIPMENT AND MATERIALS:

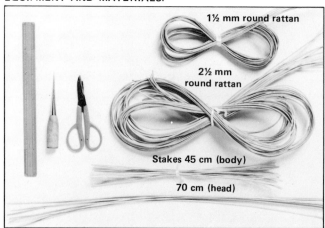

1½ mm round rattan

2½ mm round rattan

Stakes 45 cm (body)

70 cm (head)

180 g of 2½ mm round rattan, cut into 9 stakes 70 cm long for head and 17 stakes 45 cm long for body. 300 g of 1½ mm round rattan, cut into 15 stakes each 33 cm long for large leaves, 25 cm for medium and 20 cm for small.

TECHNIQUES:
Woven base; Under-two-over-two; Plain weave; Three-rod wale; Basic border A and Basic border C.

DIRECTIONS:

1. Head

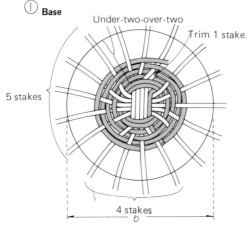

① **Base**

Under-two-over-two

Trim 1 stake.

5 stakes

4 stakes
6

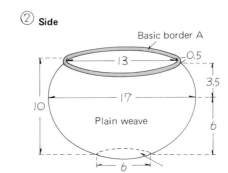

② **Side**

Basic border A

13   0.5

3.5

10

17

Plain weave

6

6

Base

Place four stakes over five to form a cross. Weave two rounds of over-four-under-five, pressing stakes. Trim one stake so that the number of stakes is uneven. Separate stakes into singles and make radial arrangement. Weave under-two-over-two.

Turn over the base. Bend stakes to a bowl shape. Work plain weave as directed. Soak remaining stakes in water and finish the edge with basic border A.

2. Body

Insert stakes of body into head and continue to weave neck and body.

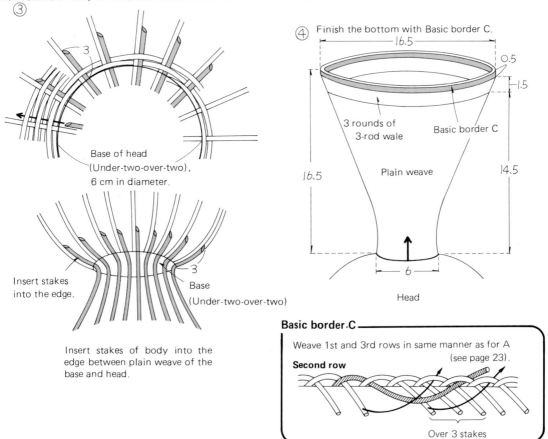

③

3

Base of head
(Under-two-over-two),
6 cm in diameter.

Insert stakes
into the edge.

3

Base
(Under-two-over-two)

Insert stakes of body into the edge between plain weave of the base and head.

④ Finish the bottom with Basic border C.

16.5

0.5

1.5

3 rounds of
3-rod wale

Basic border C

16.5

Plain weave

14.5

6

Head

Basic border C

Weave 1st and 3rd rows in same manner as for A (see page 23).

Second row

Over 3 stakes

3. Hair

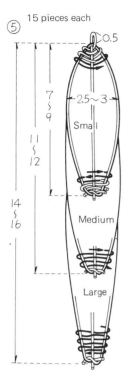

⑤ 15 pieces each

- 14～16
- 11～12
- 7～9
- 0.5
- 2.5～3
- Small
- Medium
- Large

Use 1½ mm rattan for weaver. The size and number of leaves may be adjusted depending on the way they are placed. Arrange leaves like hair for two sides of head as shown in the diagram.

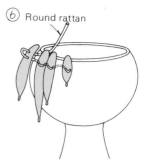

⑥ Round rattan

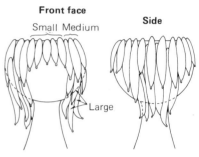

Front face

Small Medium

Side

Large

Using a well-soaked weaver, thread leaves around head, one at a time. Make front and back as shown.

Holly wreath

shown on page 17

Whole wreath is made of rattan. It is easy to make and will be a good Christmas decoration. Dye berries your favorite color.

FINISHED SIZE:

25

25 cm in diameter

TECHNIQUES:
Ring and Turk's head.

EQUIPMENT AND MATERIALS:

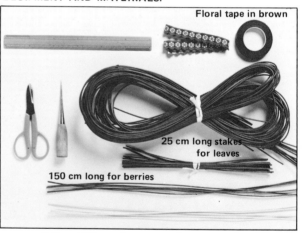

Floral tape in brown

25 cm long stakes for leaves

150 cm long for berries

130 g of 2½ mm brown round rattan, cut into 15 stakes 270 cm long for wreath and 10 stakes 25 cm long for leaves. 20 g each of 2½ mm unbleached and reddish brown round rattan, cut into 5 stakes each 150 cm long. Dye round rattan a reddish brown.

DIRECTIONS:
1. Wreath

Soak fifteen 270 cm brown rattan in water until pliable. Gather fifteen pieces together and tie one end with wire.

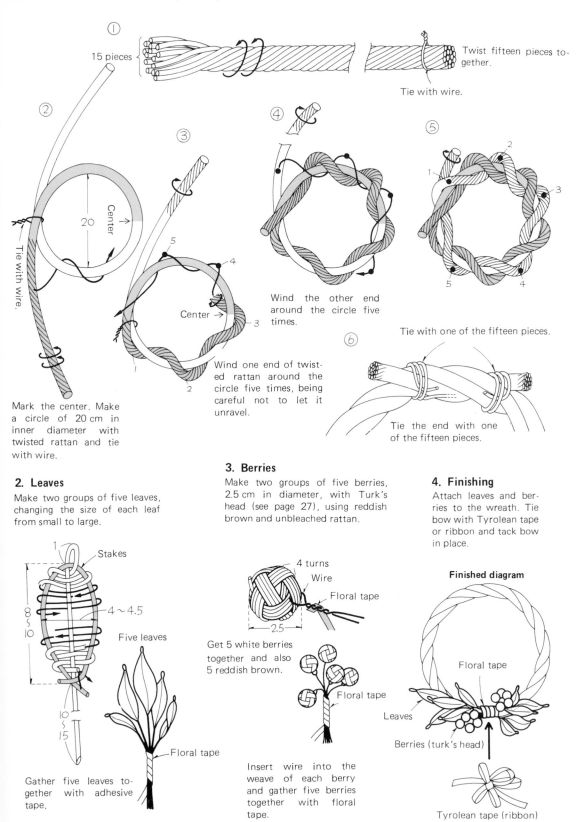

① 15 pieces

Twist fifteen pieces together.

Tie with wire.

②

Tie with wire.

20 Center

Mark the center. Make a circle of 20 cm in inner diameter with twisted rattan and tie with wire.

③

5

4

Center →

3

2

④

Wind the other end around the circle five times.

Wind one end of twisted rattan around the circle five times, being careful not to let it unravel.

⑤

1

2

3

5

4

⑥

Tie with one of the fifteen pieces.

Tie the end with one of the fifteen pieces.

2. Leaves

Make two groups of five leaves, changing the size of each leaf from small to large.

1

Stakes

8 ∼ 10

4 ∼ 4.5

Five leaves

10 ∼ 15

Floral tape

Gather five leaves together with adhesive tape.

3. Berries

Make two groups of five berries, 2.5 cm in diameter, with Turk's head (see page 27), using reddish brown and unbleached rattan.

4 turns

Wire

Floral tape

2.5

Get 5 white berries together and also 5 reddish brown.

Floral tape

Insert wire into the weave of each berry and gather five berries together with floral tape.

4. Finishing

Attach leaves and berries to the wreath. Tie bow with Tyrolean tape or ribbon and tack bow in place.

Finished diagram

Floral tape

Leaves

Berries (turk's head)

Tyrolean tape (ribbon)

shown on page 17

Jingle bells

You can make these bells with the basic basketry techniques. Make one a little bit smaller than the other. Finish the bells with Tyrolean tape to add color.

FINISHED SIZE:

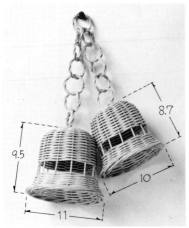

9.5 cm high and 11 cm in diameter across the bottom
8.5 cm high and 10 cm in diameter across the bottom

EQUIPMENT AND MATERIALS:

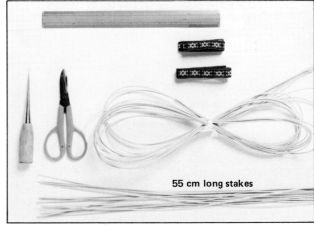

55 cm long stakes

60 g of 2 mm round rattan, cut into 7 stakes 55 cm long for one bell. Tyrolean tape, 1.5 cm by 60 cm and 1.5 cm by 55 cm.

DIRECTIONS:

1. Bell

Make two bells in the same manner except shaping stakes.

TECHNIQUES:

Overlaid cross base; Under-two-over-two; Ring; Plain weave and Basic border C.

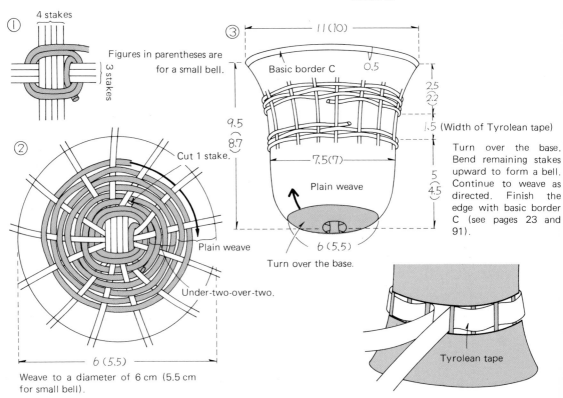

① 4 stakes
3 stakes

Figures in parentheses are for a small bell.

② Cut 1 stake.
Plain weave.
Under-two-over-two.

6 (5.5)

Weave to a diameter of 6 cm (5.5 cm for small bell).

③ 11 (10)
Basic border C   0.5
2.5 (2.2)
1.5 (Width of Tyrolean tape)
9.5 (8.7)
7.5 (7)
Plain weave
5 (4.5)
6 (5.5)
Turn over the base.

Turn over the base. Bend remaining stakes upward to form a bell. Continue to weave as directed. Finish the edge with basic border C (see pages 23 and 91).

Tyrolean tape

2. Chain for hanging

Soak 30 cm rattan in water until pliable. Insert the weaver into the bell top and make the first ring. Make second ring, connecting the first. Make third one in this way. Make the rest, connecting one after another as long as you like. Connect the last ring to the top of the bell.

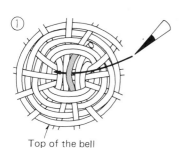

① Top of the bell

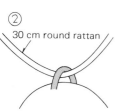

② 30 cm round rattan

Insert 30 cm rattan into the bell top.

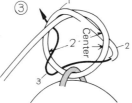

③ Mark the center of rattan and make a circle. Wind one end of rattan around the circle three times.

④ Wind the other end around the circle three times in reversing direction.

⑤ Trim both ends on a diagonal.

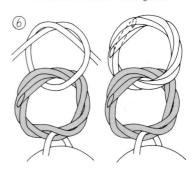

⑥ Make eleven rings, connecting one after another. Insert the weaver of the last ring into the second bell top and make ring in the same manner.

Christmas tree

shown on page 17

This is the easiest way to make Christmas tree which consists of four baskets and 5 mm center pole. Decorate the tree with colored wooden beads.

FINISHED SIZE:

27 cm high

EQUIPMENT AND MATERIALS:

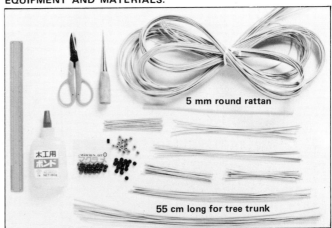

5 mm round rattan

55 cm long for tree trunk

100 g of 2½ mm round rattan, cut into 7 stakes 30 cm long, 14 additional stakes 12 cm long for A, 7 stakes 35 cm long, 14 additional stakes 14 cm long for B, 7 stakes 40 cm long, 14 additional stakes 17 cm long for C and 9 stakes 55 cm long for tree trunk. 28 cm length of 5 mm round rattan. Red, yellow and green wooden beads, 8 mm in diameter, 10 each.

TECHNIQUES:

Overlaid cross base; Plain weave; Chasing; Looped border and Trac border D.

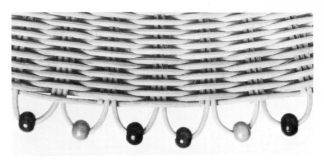

Looped border

DIRECTIONS:

1. Tree

Make A, B and C in the same manner. Place four stakes over three to form a cross. After weaving two rounds of under-three-over-four, damp stakes and shape for A, B and C.

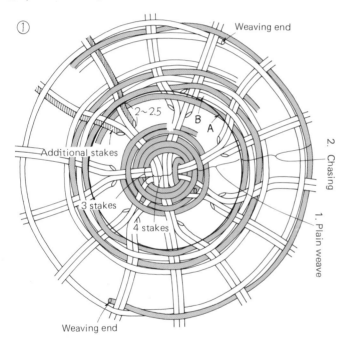

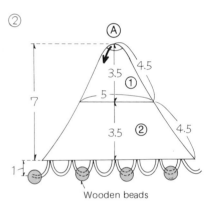

Wooden beads

After weaving section 1, insert additional stakes as shown.

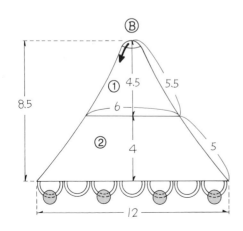

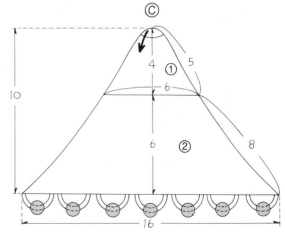

Looped border

Soak stake ends in water until pliable. Trim all stake ends to equal length. Trim left-hand stakes close to the edge. Trim right-hand stake ends on a diagonal. Insert soaked right-hand stakes into the weave parallel to the adjoining left-hand stakes. Insert wooden beads into every other stake and for A end B before finishing the edge. For C, insert beads into each stake end.

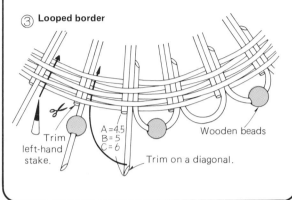

③ **Looped border**

Trim left-hand stake.

A = 4.5
B = 5
C = 6

Wooden beads

Trim on a diagonal.

3. Finishing

Insert pole into centers of A, B, C and tree trunk, using an awl for guide. Put some glue on the top of each tree before the pole is inserted.

⑤

⑥

Glue

A

B

C

4
3
4
4
27

11

16.5

2. Tree trunk

Place five stakes over four to form a cross. After weaving 4 cm in diameter, shape stakes as shown and weave over pairs of stakes. Finish the edge with trac border D (see page 55).

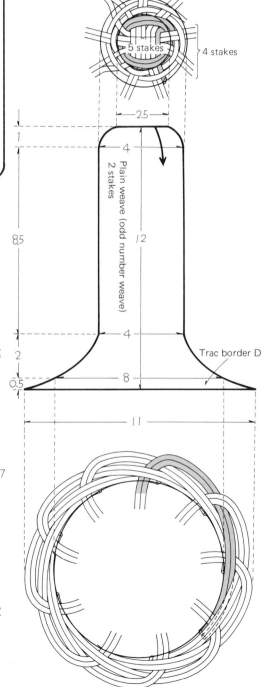

④ **Tree trunk**

5 stakes

4 stakes

2.5

1

4

Plain weave (odd number weave)
2 stakes

8.5

12

4

2

0.5

8

Trac border D

11

Metric Equivalency Chart

CONVERTING INCHES INTO MILLIMETERS AND CENTIMETERS
(slightly rounded for your convenience)

mm—millimeters   cm—centimeters

inches	mm	cm	inches	cm	inches	cm
1/8	3		7	18	29	73.5
1/4	6		8	20.5	30	76
3/8		.1	9	23	31	79
1/2		1.3	10	25.5	32	81.5
5/8		1.5	11	28	33	84
3/4		2	12	30.5	34	86.5
7/8		2.2	13	33	35	89
1		2.5	14	35.5	36	91.5
1 1/4		3.2	15	38	37	94
1 1/2		3.8	16	40.5	38	96.5
1 3/4		4.5	17	43	39	99
2		5	18	46	40	101.5
2 1/2		6.5	19	48.5	41	104
3		7.5	20	51	42	106.5
3 1/2		9	21	53.5	43	109
4		10	22	56	44	112
4 1/2		11.5	23	58.5	45	114.5
5		12.5	24	61	46	117
5 1/2		14	25	63.5	47	119.5
6		15	26	66	48	122
			27	68.5	49	124.5
			28	71	50	127

Ounce/Gram Conversions

As an aid in interchanging yarns, we have prepared the following conversion chart. It lists common yarn amounts and their ounce/gram equivalents. Please note that these conversions are approximate.

1 ounce=approximately 28 grams
40 grams=approximately 1 1/3 ounces

50 grams=approximately 1 3/4 ounces
100 grams=approximately 3 1/2 ounces